Landmarks of world literature

Scott

WAVERLEY

Landmarks of world literature

General editor: J. P. Stern

Dickens: *Bleak House* – Graham Storey
Homer: *The Iliad* – Michael Silk
Dante: *The Divine Comedy* – Robin Kirkpatrick
Balzac: *Old Goriot* – David Bellos
Mann: *Buddenbrooks* – Hugh Ridley
Homer: *The Odyssey* – Jasper Griffin
Tolstoy: *Anna Karenina* – Anthony Thorlby
Conrad: *Nostromo* – Ian Watt
Camus: *The Stranger* – Patrick McCarthy
Murasaki Shikibu: *The Tale of Genji* – Richard Bowring
Sterne: *Tristram Shandy* – Wolfgang Iser
Shakespeare: *Hamlet* – Paul A. Cantor
Stendhal: *The Red and the Black* – Stirling Haig
Pasternak: *Doctor Zhivago* – Angela Livingstone
Proust: *Swann's Way* – Sheila Stern
Pound: *The Cantos* – George Kearns
Beckett: *Waiting for Godot* – Lawrence Graver
Chaucer: *The Canterbury Tales* – Winthrop Wetherbee
Virgil: *The Aeneid* – K. W. Gransden
García Márquez: *One Hundred Years of Solitude* – Michael Wood
Cervantes: *Don Quixote* – A. J. Close
Céline: *Journey to the End of the Night* – John Sturrock
Boccaccio: *Decameron* – David Wallace
Wordsworth: *The Prelude* – Stephen Gill
Eliot: *Middlemarch* – Karen Chase
Hardy: *Tess of the d'Urbervilles* – Dale Kramer
The Bible – Stephen Prickett and Robert Barnes
Flaubert: *Madame Bovary* – Stephen Heath
Baudelaire: *Les Fleurs du mal* – F. W. Leakey
Zola: *L'Assommoir* – David Baguley
Boswell: *The Life of Johnson* – Greg Clingham
Pushkin: *Eugene Onegin* – A. D. P. Briggs
Dostoyevsky: *The Brothers Karamazov* – W. J. Leatherbarrow
Galdós: *Fortunata and Jacinta* – Harriet S. Turner
Aeschylus: *The Oresteia* – Simon Goldhill
Byron: *Don Juan* – Anne Barton
Lawrence: *Sons and Lovers* – M. H. Black
Swift: *Gulliver's Travels* – Howard Erskine-Hill
Milton: *Paradise Lost* – David Loewenstein
Augustine: *Confessions* – Gillian Clark
Scott: *Waverley* – Richard Humphrey
Mann: *Doktor Faustus* – Michael Beddow

WALTER SCOTT

Waverley

RICHARD HUMPHREY

Justus-Liebig-Universität, Gießen, Germany

CAMBRIDGE UNIVERSITY PRESS
Cambridge, New York, Melbourne, Madrid, Cape Town, Singapore, São Paulo

Cambridge University Press
The Edinburgh Building, Cambridge CB2 8RU, UK

Published in the United States of America by Cambridge University Press, New York

www.cambridge.org
Information on this title: www.cambridge.org/9780521372916

First published 1993
Re-issued in this digitally printed version 2008

A catalogue record for this publication is available from the British Library

Library of Congress Cataloguing in Publication data

Humphrey, Richard
Walter Scott – Waverley / Richard Humphrey.
p. cm. – (Landmarks of world literature)
ISBN 0 521 37291 7 (hardback) / ISBN 0 521 37888 5 (paperback)
1. Scott, Walter, Sir, 1771–1832. Waverley. 2. Jacobite Rebellion, 1745–1746 – Literature and the rebellion. 3. Historical fiction, Scottish and European – History and criticism. 4. Scotland in literature. I. Title. II. Series.
PR5322.W43H85 1993
823'.7 – dc20 92-42217 CIP

ISBN 978-0-521-37291-6 hardback
ISBN 978-0-521-37888-8 paperback

Contents

Acknowledgements

It has been a great pleasure and stimulus while working on this volume to have been able to teach *Waverley* and early European historical fiction on both sides of the Atlantic, at the *Justus-Liebig-Universität*, Gießen and in a summer as Visiting Associate Professor at the University of Wisconsin/Milwaukee.

I am most grateful also for discussions with colleagues at the 'Fact and Fiction' Conference in Waterloo (Ontario) in Autumn 1988, and to the two German funding bodies, the DFG and DAAD for funding that and other related travel.

On my several trips to Edinburgh, the staff of both the National Library and the University Library have been of great assistance and forbearance. To them and to the numerous scholars worldwide who have made the last thirty years of Scott research so invigorating an affair I am indebted for many a direction.

To Dame Jean Maxwell-Scott and to Patricia Maxwell-Scott, O.B.E., goes my especial gratitude for repeated hospitality at Abbotsford and for permission to work at length on volumes from Sir Walter's own library.

My greatest debt, however, is to the late editor of this series, supreme in encouragement and example.

Note

Numbers following quotations from *Waverley* refer to the pagination of the World's Classics paperback edition, ed. Claire Lamont, Oxford, 1986. This edition has been chosen here since it offers the 1814 text of the novel, corrected from manuscript. Although Scott's last words on *Waverley* are the emendations and appendages of the 1829 Magnum Opus edition, it is the first, 1814 version which is the landmark.

Numbers following quotations from other novels and stories by Scott refer to the *chapter* of the work concerned. The works' titles are abbreviated as follows:

BD	*The Black Dwarf*	*RG*	*Redgauntlet*
CC	*Chronicles of the Canongate*	*RR*	*Rob Roy*
GM	*Guy Mannering*	*SR*	*St Ronan's Well*
HM	*The Heart of Midlothian*	*TA*	*The Antiquary*
HW	*The Highland Widow*	*TD*	*The Two Drovers*

Numbers following quotations from other works by Scott or by other writers refer to the pagination of the editions listed below or in the Guide to Further Reading. Where more than one work by the same writer is listed, the date of the work in question is additionally given. The abbreviations are as follows:

AR '1814', *The Edinburgh Annual Register for 1814* (Edinburgh, 1816)
BA *The Border Antiquities of England and Scotland* (London and Edinburgh, 1814)
CP Review of the *Culloden Papers*, *The Quarterly Review*, 14 (1816)
J *The Journal of Sir Walter Scott*, ed. W.E.K. Anderson
JH Review of *The Life and Works of John Home*, *The Quarterly Review*, 36, 1827
L *The Letters of Sir Walter Scott*, ed. H.J.C. Grierson
MB *Minstrelsy of the Scottish Border* (Edinburgh, 1802)
MM *Letters of Malachi Malagrowther* (Edinburgh and London, 1826)
PL *Paul's Letters to his Kinsfolk* (Edinburgh, 1816)
RS *Description of the Regalia of Scotland* (Edinburgh, 1819)

Chronology

	Europe and Beyond	*Scotland*	*Scott*
1740–8	War of the Austrian Succession		
1745		Last Jacobite Rising (the Forty-five): Battle of Prestonpans and march to Derby	Family briefly divided over Rising
1746	*Ascanius* and other fictions of the Forty-five	Battle of Culloden. Penal laws against non-established religions	Distant relatives among those killed
1747		Proscription Act forbids wearing of highland dress. Jacobite estates forfeited	
1748	Remains of Pompeii discovered. Montesquieu, *L'Esprit des Lois*. Richardson, *Clarissa*	Hume, *An Enquiry Concerning Human Understanding*. Smollett, *Roderick Random*	
1749	Fielding, *Tom Jones*		
1750		One-eighth of population urban. Half America's tobacco crop now exported to Glasgow	
1753	British Museum (first public museum) founded		
1754–6		Joseph Black discovers carbonic gas, carbonic dioxide	

1754–61		Hume, *History of England*	
1756–63	Seven Years War ('Great War for Empire')		
1758	Sterne, *Tristram Shandy*	Adam Smith, *Theory of Moral Sentiments*	Marriage of parents – Walter Scott, Writer to the Signet (solicitor), and Anne Rutherford, daughter of Edinburgh professor of medicine
1759		Carron ironworks established. Robert Burns born	Scotts begin family on Anchor Close, off High Street, Edinburgh
1760	Beginning of Gaelic vernacular revival	Black defines difference between heat and temperature	
1761		'Ossian', *Fingal, an Ancient Epic Poem*	
1762	Rousseau, *Le Contrat social*	Cast iron converted into malleable at Carron works	
1764	Walpole, *Castle of Otranto*	Watt invents the condenser	
1765	Percy, *Reliques of Ancient English Poetry*		
1766		James Craig's plan for Edinburgh's New Town chosen	
1767		Ferguson, *Essay on the History of Civil Society*	Family moves to the College Wynd, Old Town
1768	Cook's first voyage of discovery		
1769	Napoleon Bonaparte born	Watt patents steam engine	
1770	Rousseau, *Confessions*	Wave of emigration from the Highlands. Act of Parliament to improve the Broomielaw, Glasgow	

1771	Arkwright opens first spinning mill in England	*Encyclopaedia Britannica* founded in Edinburgh. Mackenzie, *The Man of Feeling*	Scott born on the College Wynd – the ninth of twelve children, of whom only six survive infancy
1772–3			Attack of poliomyelitis leaves him lame in his right leg
1773	Boston Tea Party. Goethe, *Götz von Berlichingen*	Priestley discovers oxygen. Montboddo, *Of the Origin and Progress of Languages*	
1773–5			Sent for health to Sandy-Knowe, in the Borders
1774	Suppression of Pugachev Rising. Goethe, *Die Leiden des jungen Werther*	Kames, *Sketches of the History of Man.* General Register House, Edinburgh, begun	
1775	Highland Society of London founded		Goes for a cure to Bath; visits London
1775–83	American War of Independence		
1776	American Declaration of Independence	Adam Smith, *Wealth of Nations*	Family moves to George Square, Old Town
1777		Robertson, *History of America*	First visit to Prestonpans and meeting with George Constable, *raconteur* of the Forty-five
1779	Spain declares war on Britain	First cotton spinning-mill (at Penicuik)	
1779–83			Attends High School, Edinburgh
1780		Antiquarian Society of Scotland founded	

1781			Comes to know Alexander Stuart of Invernayle, major *raconteur* of the Forty-five and source for *Waverley*
1782		Proscription Act repealed. Highland Clearances begin. Antiquaries' Musaeum established. 8 newspapers in Scotland	
1783	Peace of Versailles determines shape of future British Empire	*Glasgow Herald* founded	Stays with aunt at Kelso. Discovers Percy's *Reliques*
1783–6			Attends classes at Edinburgh University
1784	Herder, *Ideen zu einer Philosophie der Geschichte der Menschheit*	Watt invents double-acting engine. Jacobite estates returned. Highland Society founded	
1785		Boswell, *Tour to the Hebrides*	
1785–6			Haemorrhage: break in education, long convalescence at Kelso
1786		Burns, *Poems, Chiefly in the Scottish Dialect*	Apprenticed to father. First visit to Highlands
1787			Falls in love with 'Jessie from Kelso': love poetry
1788	First colony in Australia	Charles Edward Stuart (Bonnie Prince Charlie) dies. Hutton, *Theory of the Earth*	
1789	Storming of the Bastille. Constituent Assembly in France		'On the Origins of the Feudal System'. 'On the Origin of the Scandinavian Mythology'

1789–92			Again attends Edinburgh University
1790	Burke, *Reflections on the Revolution in France*	Water-powered spinning introduced. 27 newspapers in Scotland	
1791	Paine, *Rights of Man*		
1792		Penal laws repealed. Severe clearances – 'The Year of the Sheep'. General Convention of Scottish Friends of the People	Becomes Member of Faculty of Advocates. Collects ballads in Liddesdale. Falls in love with Williamina Belches
1793	Louis XVI executed. Reign of Terror in France. Napoleonic Wars begin. Louvre (first national museum) founded	Convention leaders transported	Visit to Tullibody, Doune castle, Glamis
1794	Radcliffe, *The Mysteries of Udolpho*		
1795	Directory in France. British take the Cape		
1796	Napoleon's Italian campaign	Death of Burns	Translations of Bürger – *The Chase* and *William and Helen* – first (anonymous) publication. Williamina spurns him
1797	Threat of Napoleonic invasion of Britain		Co-founder and Secretary of Edinburgh Light Dragoons. Marries Charlotte Charpentier
1798	Napoleon's Egyptian campaign. Wordsworth and Coleridge, *Lyrical Ballads*		Moves to 39, (North) Castle Street, New Town

1799			Publishes translation of Goethe's *Götz* (under own name). Contributes to *Tales of Terror*. Death of father. Daughter (Charlotte) born. Becomes Sheriff-Depute of Selkirkshire
1800	Maria Edgeworth, *Castle Rackrent*	Expansion of woollen tweed manufacture in Borders	*The Eve of Saint John*
1801		Telford surveys potential of Highlands	Contributes to Lewis's *Tales of Wonder*. Son (Walter) born
1802	Peace with France	*Edinburgh Review* founded	
1802–3			*The Minstrelsy of the Scottish Border*. Daughter (Anne) born
1803	War with France resumes	Commission to open up Highlands established	
1804	Napoleon crowned Emperor		Takes country house at Ashetiel; visited there by Wordsworth
1805	Battles of Trafalgar, Austerlitz		*The Lay of the Last Minstrel* – an immediate success bringing fame and profit. Becomes partner in Ballantyne printing company. Son (Charles) born. First chapters of *Waverley* (?)
1806	Battle of Jena		*Ballads and Lyrical Pieces*. Becomes a Principal Clerk of Session
1807	Hegel, *Phänomenologie des Geistes*		Concludes Strutt's historical romance, *Queenhoo-Hall*. Secretary to Parliamentary Commission for Improvement of Scottish Jurisprudence

1808			*Marmion* nets 1,000 guineas in advance. Edition of Dryden. Helps found *Quarterly Review*. Work on *Waverley* (?)
1810	Kleist, *Michael Kohlhaas*		*The Lady of the Lake*. Work on *Waverley* (?)
1811			Buys Clarty Hole – the beginnings of Abbotsford. *The Vision of Don Roderick*
1812	Napoleon's retreat from Moscow. Byron, *Childe Harold's Pilgrimage*	Weavers' strike in Glasgow and West	Move to Abbotsford
1813	Battle of Nations at Leipzig	Gillespie's master plan for Edinburgh's West End	*Rokeby*. Declines Poet Laureateship. Made Freeman of City of Edinburgh. Ballantyne helped out of financial troubles by Constable. *Waverley* resumed
1814	Napoleon abdicates. Britain celebrates peace in Europe (7 July)	Severe clearances – 'The Year of the Burnings'	Edition of Swift. *Waverley* (7 July) – another major success: profits of £2,100 by end of year. Agrees to write essay on 'Romance', contributes 'Chivalry' and 'Drama' to *Encyclopaedia Britannica*
1814–17			*The Border Antiquities of England and Scotland*
1815	The Hundred Days. Battle of Waterloo. Holy Alliance	Glenfinnan monument to the Forty-five	*The Lord of the Isles. Guy Mannering*. Visits battlefield at Waterloo and Paris

1816			*Paul's Letters to his Kinsfolk. The Antiquary. Tales of My Landlord*, first series (*The Black Dwarf* and *Old Mortality*). '1814'
1817		*The Scotsman* founded	First grave stomach disorder
1818	Congress of Aix-la-Chapelle		*Rob Roy. Tales of My Landlord*, second series (*The Heart of Midlothian*)
1819	Peterloo Massacre. Carlsbad Decrees. Singapore taken. Irving, *Rip van Winkle*		*Tales of My Landlord*, third series (*The Bride of Lammermoor* and *A Legend of Montrose*). *Ivanhoe* sells 10,000 copies in a fortnight. Death of mother
1819–26			*The Provincial Antiquities of Scotland*
1820	Liberal revolt in Spain	'Radical War' in West – last rising against Union. Celtic Society founded	*The Monastery. The Abbot*
1821	Greek War of Independence. Cooper, *The Spy*. Adolphus, *Letters to Richard Heber*	One-third of population now urban. Galt, *The Ayreshire Legatees, Annals of the Parish*	*Kenilworth*
1822	Congress of Vienna discusses Greece, Spain. Hegel first lectures on philosophy of history	George IV visits Scotland. Second New Town, Edinburgh started. Caledonian Canal opened	*The Pirate. The Fortunes of Nigel. Peveril of the Peak*. Essay on 'Romance'. Part-organizer of George IV's visit
1823	Alexis, *Die Geächteten*. Cooper, *The Pioneers*. Hugo, *Han d'Islande*. Alexis, 'The Romances of Walter Scott'	Galt, *The Entail*	*Quentin Durward. St Ronan's Well.* First symptoms of apoplexy

1824	Anglo-Burmese Wars. Death of Byron	Hogg, *Confessions of a Justified Sinner*	*Redgauntlet*
1825	Decembrist uprising in Russia	Widespread business failures	*Tales of the Crusaders* (*The Betrothed* and *The Talisman*). Begins *Journal*
1826	Cooper, *The Last of the Mohicans*. Tieck, *Der Aufruhr in den Cevennen*. De Vigny, *Cinq-Mars*	Galt, *The Last of the Lairds*	Collapse of Ballantyne, Constable: Scott left bankrupt. Sells 39 Castle Street. Wife dies. *Letters of Malachi Malagrowther*. *Woodstock*
1827	Treaty of London. Manzoni, The *Betrothed*		Public acknowledgement of authorship of Waverley Novels. *Life of Napoleon Buonaparte*. *Chronicles of the Canongate*, first series (*The Highland Widow, The Two Drovers, The Surgeon's Daughter*)
1828			*Tales of a Grandfather*, first series. *Chronicles of the Canongate*, first series (*The Fair Maid of Perth*)
1829	Balzac, *Les Chouans*	Thomas Graham formulates law on diffusion of gases	*Anne of Geierstein*. *Tales of a Grandfather*, second series. Magnum Series of Waverley Novels
1830	Liberal revolt across Europe. Greece declared independent.		*Tales of a Grandfather*, third series. Electioneering before hostile crowds. Paralytic attack. Apoplectic attack
1831	Mazzini launches Young Italy. Hugo, *Notre Dame de Paris*	Ross determines position of magnetic North Pole	*Tales of a Grandfather*, fourth series. Health compels voyage to Mediterranean. Government supplies frigate
1832	First Reform Bill. Death of Goethe	Reform Act (Scotland) passed. Galt, *The Member*	*Tales of My Landlord*, fourth series. Returns to die at Abbotsford. Debts now almost paid. Death (21 September)

Introduction

A landmark of literature is a work from which successions of readers – or subsequent authors, and hence literary historians – take their bearings. It may crystallize an experience or epitomize an age. It may initiate a genre or exemplify a mode. It may influence intellectual life or even enlarge the readership of literature and the possibilities of publishing. Or, in a rare instance, it may do all of these things. Such a rare instance is Walter Scott's *Waverley* (1814).

The sheer number and quality of writers who took their bearings from *Waverley* would ensure its position in literary history. One has only to study the plots, casts and themes of the cream of European novelists in the 1820s and 1830s – from Balzac to Stendhal, from Pushkin to Gogol, from Manzoni to Tieck – to discover that this story set in and around the 1745 Jacobite rising in Scotland not only struck a chord all over Europe: it dictated much of the subsequent score too. On his death in 1832, *The Times* could justly call Scott's name and work 'not only British but European – not only European but universal'.

Such emulation is accorded only to innovation. There had been countless novels set in the past before. But with its new sense for the qualitative difference between present and past, and with its new awareness of causation and interconnection within that changing past, *Waverley* was more. In 1832, the *Caledonian Mercury* could hail Scott as the 'Columbus of fiction'. And as early as 1826 and 1827, the German critics Alexis and Menzel had named the territory he opened up: Scott was the discoverer of the 'genuine historical novel', the 'founder of the historical novel as a literary species *sui generis*'.

From *Waverley*, however, the above novelists derived more than the manifold possibilities of a new genre. In *Waverley*, wrote Tieck, bygone Scotland is 'so depicted that one is veritably living with all the people'; in Scott, wrote Pushkin, 'we get to know past times as though we were living a day-to-day life in them ourselves'. And the earliest reviews abound in such words as 'accurate', 'faithful', 'minute' and 'correct'. For *Waverley* contains passages of social description and analysis which are among the earliest examples – and exemplars – of conscientious realism. And here emulation is not restricted to *historical* novelists, nor does it restrict them to *historical* novels. Balzac's historical novel *Les Chouans* is one facet of Scott's influence; his *Comédie humaine* is another.

This imaginative sympathy for the otherness of the past and this successful recreation, over a broad social spectrum, of the vitality of the past did not go unnoticed among those writers traditionally entrusted with the past. 'Scott', declared Macaulay in 1828, 'has used those fragments of truth which historians have thrown behind them in a manner which may well excite their envy'. Even the austere Ranke confessed that Scott 'played a principal part in awakening my sympathy for the actions and passions of past ages'. And again these voices were echoed all over Europe. So much so that, writes Croce, 'no one can write a sound history of historical writing in the nineteenth century without giving generous credit to Walter Scott'. Of course, Scott's work as a whole is the testator here. But if subsequent historiography does turn away from 'drum and trumpet' reports, does portray the political and the social in the 'inseparable conjunction and intermixture' Macaulay called for, then it is to *Waverley*, in which this shift is first and signally exhibited, that the legacy must be traced.

This broad influence would have been unlikely had *Waverley* not been what it *also* was: a landmark in publishing. Capturing the imagination of Edinburgh on its appearance on 7 July 1814, selling out within five weeks, finding six thousand buyers within six months, going through eight editions in five years and into at least six European languages within thirteen years, *Waverley* opened, in the words of Richard Altick, a 'new era in fiction'. And now that *Waverley* has long since given its name not only to Scott's 'Waverley Novels' (1814–31), but to a town, a railway station, hotels, bookstores, note-paper, the Waverley pen (that came 'as a Boon and a Blessing to men'), a record label, a biscuit factory, knick-knacks and whatnot, it can be difficult to see the book for the ballyhoo. Nothing obscures like success.

Two things, however, must be remembered. Firstly, *Waverley* was not just a bestseller: it was the *first* bestseller, or, in the more precise phrase of A.N. Wilson, 'the first bestselling novel in the modern sense'. And secondly, this bestseller attracted the best readers – and then held them.

It would not have *created* a broad novel-reading public if it had not enacted conflicts essential to its age. As Coleridge recognized as early as 1820, Scott dramatizes 'the contest between the two great moving principles of social humanity' – 'religious adherence to the past and the ancient' versus 'the mighty instincts of progression and free agency'. And within that struggle, ever-renewed in, and ever speaking to, our own age of exponential change, are two further conflicts equally central to its age and ours: the conflict between tight-bonded community and more diffuse society, between *Gemeinschaft* and *Gesellschaft*; and that between dominant, domineering nation and prized neighbour.

But equally, Scott could not have held such *distinguished* readers if these conflicts had not memorably found the appropriate form. As literature – declared the other European Olympian, Goethe, in 1828 – *Waverley* could 'without hesitation, be set beside the best works that have ever been written in this world.' As history – G.M. Trevelyan could state as late as 1937 – *Waverley* was 'the best history book on the '45, considered as a social phenomenon in its particular time and place'. And what finally cements the achievement of the work is that it both moves on to new forms and reflects on those it leaves behind: it is a negotiation between romance and realism, ballad and novel, old history and new. Here, in other words, is a fundamental and pivotal text of the modern age. *Waverley* does not just 'add a stone to the cairn': it is a cairn in its own right – a fourfold landmark of literature.

This brief volume cannot hope to map in detail all the

territory such a landmark surveys and serves. Geographically, temporally and intellectually the area is considerably broader than the above sketch. Topographically it contains some notoriously difficult terrain – the marshlands of realism, the disputed marches between novel and history, the slough of whether the historical novel *is* a genre *sui generis*. Nevertheless, the dual perspective required by the present series – looking not only from monument to territory but back again – can hope to add fresh understanding. Carlyle, mapping the same ground in 1838, wrote that *Waverley* was 'an event memorable in the annals of British Literature; in the annals of British Bookselling thrice and four times memorable'. The present author would be happy if he managed to show that *Waverley* was more memorable in other annals – those of *Scottish* society and thought, of Napoleonic Europe, of European and world literature, and, not least, of our own concerns.

Chapter 1

Scott's changing world and the making of *Waverley*

1 The Napoleonic years

O who, that shared them, ever shall forget
  The emotions of the spirit-rousing time ...

The Lord of the Isles, VI

Napoleonic Europe is to the historical novel what ancient Greece is to tragic drama: both one of its enduring themes and its birthplace. Not only was the turbulence of those years to attract the cream of historical novelists, from Balzac, Stendhal and Thackeray through Tolstoy and Pérez Galdós to Fontane, Hardy and Conrad, but *Waverley* itself, the inaugurator of the genre, was begun, Scott states, in 1805, just weeks after Trafalgar (or, others suggest, around 1808–10, with the Peninsular War in full flow), resumed in Autumn 1813, on the eve of the Battle of Nations at Leipzig and published in July 1814 less than a year before Waterloo. Indeed, on its day of publication, Thursday, 7 July 1814, the British nation was officially – if prematurely – celebrating peace in Europe.

What a context! But – is it one? Does it in any way help to account for *Waverley*, and if so, for how much and why?

The circumstantial evidence linking Scott (1771–1832) and Bonaparte is, to be sure, strong. After all, the two men shared the same birthday – Napoleon being just two years Scott's senior – and so took their respective *gradus ad Parnassum* in step. As the opening chronology details, Scott became a student and advocate between Revolution and 9 Thermidor, a translator and published poet between Directory and 18 Brumaire, a published anthologer and renowned poet between Consulate and Austerlitz, and an editor, laureate nominee and lauded historical novelist (and owner-builder of his country seat at Abbotsford) between then and St Helena. The twenty-five central years of his life thus spanned wars which, if not the bloodiest Europe had known, were unprecedented in their extent, territorial implications, institutional and social impact and sheer cost. Chronology and common sense alone might lead one to echo Goethe, who, reviewing Scott's life in 1827, exclaimed, 'What must he have experienced living so in such a time?' Only, a conjuncture is not a connection.

Again, to link the two men would not be anachronistic. On the contrary, it became part of the rhetoric of the age: Balzac mentioned them in one breath; Henry Cockburn wrote that Scott's 'advances were like the conquests of Napoleon: each new achievement overshadowing the last' (196); and on Scott's death, *The Athenaeum* even likened the emergence of *Waverley* to the Hundred Days. Only, nice conceits are not connections either.

And again, to link the new genre itself to the Napoleonic upheavals is a long-standing theoretical position. In an important essay of 1827, 'Walter Scott and His Century', the German critic Menzel sees the genre as 'the true child of its time', reflecting the national struggles, *levées en masse* and democratic stirrings of the age. Such thoughts are echoed in the now best-known sociology of the genre, Lukács's *The Historical Novel* (1937, tr. 1962) – which argues that the genre emerged not least because of 'the French Revolution, the revolutionary wars and the rise and fall of Napoleon, which for the first time made history a *mass experience*, and moreover on a European scale' (20) – but neither Lukács nor Menzel give what such theory requires, namely biographical evidence of the link between that experience and the Scott of *Waverley.* Contentions, however, are not connections either.

Now, the connections *can* be made. His earliest biographer, Lockhart, shows Scott helping form a cavalry defence unit in 1797, charting the campaigns closely, especially from 1809 on, celebrating allied successes with his household and, in 1813, illumining his Edinburgh windows with candles on Wellington's entering Paris. In 1815, Scott went hot-foot to Paris himself via the battlefield at Waterloo and a year later, in a lengthy but little-known essay entitled '1814', published in the *Edinburgh Annual Register* for that year, wrote: 'Neither will the sensations which we have felt during this remarkable era be ever erased from the minds on which they were so powerfully impressed' (*AR* 366).

More telling is that '1814' is by no means an isolated incursion into the Napoleonic years. Scott's extensive correspondence offers a running commentary on them – especially from 1808 on – with Bonaparte both wondered at as a general 'possessing the genius and talents of an Eastern conqueror' (*L* III, 451), as a figure who has attained 'the most unbounded authority ever vested in the hands of one man' (*L* III, 440), and deplored as an 'evil demon' and 'tyrannical monster' (*L* II, 135), as 'the arch enemy of mankind' and the 'Devil' incarnate (*L* III, 440). During the Wars, both *Marmion* (1808) and the *Vision of Don Roderick* (1811) allude to them (the latter's profits going to aid their victims). And afterwards the 1815 trip gives rise to *Paul's Letters to His Kinsfolk* (1816), a travelogue through war-racked Europe; his third historical novel, *The Antiquary* (1816), revolves around a rumoured Napoleonic invasion of Scotland; and for some two years in the mid-1820s he toils over a seven-volume *Life of Napoleon Buonaparte* (1827).

More telling again, however, is that *Waverley* itself is a novel of extended journeys and military encounters, of nations in conflict and leaders in contention, of the civilian on the battlefield and of history coming home to him and others – a novel which could understandably be seen as a response to the Napoleonic age, could be seen in the terms Menzel proposes. Indeed the very language of the campaigns finds its way into the novel, a crowd of irate villagers being termed a 'levy en masse' (153), and the highlanders once being said to have 'bivouacked' (116) on the heather.

Thus although Scott would not, like Balzac, proclaim, 'What he could not complete with the sword I shall accomplish with the pen', there are grounds for saying that by 1815 Napoleon had for twenty years 'ridden Scott's imagination' (Buchan, 147). If Romantic literature is indeed 'the sum total of the ways in which man's self-awareness was affected by the Revolutionary-Napoleonic disruption' (Talmon, 136), then Scott is on these grounds also a Romantic.

And yet for all this evidence - circumstantial, biographical and textual – those who would view the Napoleonic years as the sole or prime context in which *Waverley* is to be understood must still face two awkward objections. They must explain how, from Carlyle through Grierson to Daiches, strong accounts of Scott have been written which mention this context scarcely or not at all. And that done, they must also explain why Scott – unlike his illustrious successors listed at the outset – scarcely touches on these years in historical fiction. The Napoleonic years thesis might explain why a genre with such topoi arose: it cannot explain why the first exemplar of the genre is sited not in the Napoleonic years but in the farther past, and written both about and in a European country *relatively* little affected by those Wars – Scotland.

Waverley, one must conclude, though born in the Napoleonic years, cannot be accounted for solely in terms of them, and so other terms must now be sought.

2 The Age of History and the Scottish Enlightenment

> ... which has perhaps at no period been equalled, considering the depth and variety of talent it embraced and concentrated.
>
> *Guy Mannering*, XXXIX

For many, these other terms are offered not so much by historians as by historians of history. From R. G. Collingwood through Sir Herbert Butterfield to Foucault the period of Scott's life has been seen as the threshold of modern historiography and whatever the cause of *that* development – be it social change, the collapse of the theodicy or the comparative 'de-historicization' of Man – it is plausible to see that emergence as a precondition of the parallel emergence of historical fiction. A prominent exponent of this view, Avrom Fleishman, argues:

> Only when the changes in men's predominant activities had begun to reflect themselves in the ways in which they conceived history did the literary expression of a sense of history begin to burgeon, only then did it take the peculiar form of the historical novel. (17)

Waverley so considered is thus the child less of the Napoleonic Age than of the Age of History.

Here too the circumstantial evidence appears compelling. The mid-eighteenth century was a time in which philosophers turned historian, or historians, philosopher, the resulting *philosophie de l'histoire* presuming to explicate what society should be from what it had (or had not) been. Montesquieu's *L'Esprit des lois* (1748) Voltaire's *Essai sur les moeurs* (1756), and Rousseau's *Contrat social* (1762) are just the best known of a stream of works aiming not just to describe society but to change it. They were accompanied, moreover, by a flood of popular histories – with universal histories especially in vogue – so that in 1769 David Hume could claim that 'History is now the favourite reading'. By Scott's birth, book catalogues confirm, no discipline was more read, written and written *about* than history.

Moreover, as the very name of Hume suggests, this was a development which did have a specifically, even a predominantly, Scottish element. The years 1740 to 1790 saw Edinburgh emerge as the justly dubbed 'Athens of the North', and much of the renowned work of this Scottish Enlightenment had a firm historical direction. In philosophy, Hume's *Treatise of Human Nature* (1739–40), in economics, Adam Smith's *Inquiry into the Nature and Causes of the Wealth of Nations* (1776), in sociology, Adam Ferguson's *Essay on the History of Civil Society* (1767), in linguistic anthropology, Lord Monboddo's *Of the Origin and Progress of Languages* (1773–92) not to mention in history itself, Hume's *History of England* (1754), William Robertson's histories of Scotland, America and ancient India and Lord Kames's *Sketches of the History of Man* (1774) – there is scarcely an academic discipline to which the Scottish mind did not make a major European, and origin-oriented contribution. Small wonder Hegel was soon to write that 'English philosophizing is restricted to Edinburgh and Glasgow'!

Nor is there any difficulty in establishing a connection between this historical ferment and Scott, the first twenty-five years of whose life coincide with, and are spent increasingly among the households and clubs, the literati and 'eaterati', of Edinburgh's Golden Age. In his first *Memoirs* (1808) Scott admittedly writes of his early years that 'names, dates and the other technicalities of history escaped me in a most melancholy degree' and that 'the philosophy of history, a much more important subject, was also a sealed book at this period of my life' (Hewitt, 1981, 27). Among his earliest known writings, however – listed in the chronology – are two 1789 papers 'On the Origins of ...' and, as his vast and beautifully preserved library shows, the seals of *philosophie de l'histoire* were later broken. Almost all the above works, Scottish and continental, were present on his shelves, and cheek by jowl with them – in what is perhaps the best relief map we have of this remarkable mind – was a huge congeries of histories, renowned and recondite, from Hume to Gibbon, from Froissart to Mably, and beyond. In his second historical novel, *Guy Mannering* (1815) Scott refers to Robertson, 'our historian of Scotland, of the Continent, and of America' and gives his hero letters of introduction not only to him but to Hume, Ferguson and Adam Smith into the bargain (*GM* 39).

From this Enlightenment context come four things essential to *Waverley*. First and foremost is its broader scope of historical enquiry – *Waverley* being famed in its day for its 'wider sweep'. Further there is its sense of progress and 'improvement' – a key term in Scott's oeuvre. Then from Ferguson (with whose family the Scotts were friends), come, thirdly, the very tone and terms in which the 'rude culture' of the highlanders will be described. And finally, from Hume, (who stated that the 'first quality of an historian is to be true and impartial' and whom Rousseau described as *le seul historien qui jamais ait écrit avec impartialité*) comes an advance towards balanced history. But for the new scope and tone of Golden Age history there might have been no long journey for Edward to make, no 'rude' highlanders for him to encounter, no wavering to be done between his cause and theirs.

Above all, however, Edward's journey could not have been what it also and decisively is – not just a *geographical* journey to a far-flung region, but a *temporal* journey back to an earlier stage of society. One of the major new historiographic topoi of the late Enlightenment was an awareness of the co-existence in *one and the same age* of civilizations at *different stages* of development. This is present in Robertson's *History of America* (1777), of which Edmund Burke wrote that 'now the great map of mankind is unrolled at once, and there is no state or gradation of barbarism, and no mode of refinement, which we have not at the same moment under our view'. And like so much of turn-of-the-century history, the topos – now known as the 'simultaneity of the non-simultaneous' – is graphically stated, contextualized and popularized in Schiller's inaugural lecture as Professor of History at Jena in 1789:

> The discoveries which our European mariners have made in distant oceans and on far-flung coasts offer us a spectacle as instructive as it is entertaining. They show us peoples on a great variety of levels of education, grouped around us like children of different ages around an adult, reminding him by their example what he himself once was and whence he came.

Waverley is the first novel of this spectacle – but all the more instructive in that its ages and stages are found not by a mariner to far-flung shores but by a traveller within 'civilized' Britain.

Between Waverley's travels and those of the *philosophes* there is, however, a key difference: whereas they traverse the 'great map of mankind' unrolled in the present, Edward leads us to differing stages of Man in an age which is *itself also different* from that present. In order to take that further step, in order to write a novel about the pastness of the past, Scott, like his library, had to go beyond the Enlightenment – to Romanticism.

Enlightenment history had the drawback of its merit: in search of the 'constant and universal principles of human nature' (Hume) it was not so sensitive to the uniqueness of past ages. But precisely to doubt this 'conception of human nature as something uniform and unchanging' was, Collingwood (1946, 84) has argued, one of the achievements of Romanticism, and the essential difference between Scott and Hume. The doubt was voiced through an imaginative sympathy for the past, which Butterfield calls 'almost a new dimension added to our thinking – there is such a remarkable lack of it in the Renaissance and even in much of the eighteenth century' (17).

Moreover, he too mentions Scott in this regard. For, although Scott may have derived the historical sense from Goethe's *Götz von Berlichingen* (1773) – Carlyle named 'Götzism' and 'Werterism' as the two main literary infections of the age, and Scott certainly caught the former, producing a (rather inaccurate) translation of the drama in 1799 – he was soon himself here the major purveyor. As the historian Dame C. V. Wedgwood has written: 'It was just this imaginative effort which the Romantics forced upon – or bequeathed to – historical scholarship. The foremost figure in this development was Sir Walter Scott' (27).

This imaginative effort marks off *Waverley* both from earlier novels about the past and from the novel at large. The eighteenth-century novel is noted for a 'background of particularized time and place' (Watt, 22); *Waverley*, however, sets time and place in the past and in a past acknowledged different from the present. Because the past is different, the imaginative effort is required. But because the past is past, the imagining will bring with it knowledge which, in that past, was long in the future. The major result is indicated in Scott's full title, which – not chosen without 'grave and solid deliberation' (1) – is a nice advance on the *Vincent; or, Virtue Vindicated* mode of the time. *Waverley, or, 'Tis Sixty Years Since* makes clear that this new novel is potentially two things – past experience and later knowledge: past experience for the characters, later knowledge for their author and readers. This temporal duality is at the core both of *Waverley*'s plot and of what in Tolstoy will become the genre's major contribution to philosophy of history – an insight into the two lives we all live, free and determined.

To see *Waverley* as a child of the Age of History is thus to see it as the beneficiary both of the Enlightenment and of Romanticism. The two legacies can be traced even further into the very fabric of the *Waverley* plaid. In the opening chapter, where Scott speaks of a 'great book of Nature, the same through a thousand editions' and able to impart 'moral lessons' (5) two threads of the Enlightenment come through – its uniformitarianism, or belief in an unchanging human nature, and its *historia magistra vitae*, the use of the past as preceptor of the present. But in Scott's analysis of the highland chieftain's character as one 'which could only have been acquired Sixty Years since' (91), and in the ubiquitous rhetoric of 'of the period', 'of these times', 'now universal', a stronger weave becomes dominant – that of a Romantic feeling backwards into a past felt to be unique.

Taken separately, therefore, these first two overall contexts – the Napoleonic and the historiographic – account for a fair amount of *Waverley*. Taken together, however, they account for one thing more. As Carl Becker, in his fine history of the historiography of the age, has argued, it was precisely the post-Napoleonic world which needed one final offering of post-Enlightenment history – a stabilizing sense of continuity:

> After twenty-five years of revolution and international war, most people felt the need of stabilizing society; and the most satisfactory rationalization of this need was presented by those historians and jurists who occupied themselves with social origins, who asked the question, How did society, especially the particular society of this or that nation, come to be what it is? (96)

That question and the sense of bearings its answer gives are a further part of the appeal of *Waverley* in 1814. Edward journeys in 1745 not least so that his first readers can retrace the journeys their own lives have taken in the interim – journeys which, in the famous last image of the novel are seen as a reassuring drift 'down the stream of a deep and smooth river' (340).

So another meaningful way of narrating the stream of Scott's own life would be to say he was born just a year after David Hume wrote proudly of Scotland: 'I believe that this is the historical Age and this the historical Nation'; that he lived through and fostered the emergence of what we could now call 'history'; and that he wrote more than half the Waverley Novels while Hegel was giving the lectures now known as his (equally stabilizing) *Philosophy of History*.

Yet for all the ground this second context covers, it too leaves one with some way to go: while explaining why and in what manner Scott the novelist turned to the past, and while suggesting why he might turn to a Scottish past, it cannot yet explain why he turned to the *particular* Scottish past of the 1745 uprising.

3 Changing Scotland

And o'er the landscape as I look,
Nought do I see unchanged remain

Marmion, IV, 24

In introducing his river of time image Scott makes the famous claim that 'There is no European nation which, within the course of half a century, or little more, has undergone so complete a change as this kingdom of Scotland'. To the modern reader this may seem unlikely: after all, Europe at large was in the grip of the 'Age of Revolution' and in the Industrial Revolution England had been in the van. Scott's claim, however, is both echoed by contemporaries and corroborated by modern historians: 'In no country, it may be safely said,' wrote John Anderson in 1825 in a prize essay on the 'State of Society and Knowledge in the Highlands', 'is there a parallel of so rapid a change'; and, making the comparison with England, the economic historian T.M. Devine has written:

> from the later eighteenth century the break with the past seems to have been sharper and more decisive north of the Border and the consequent social change more disruptive and, in some cases, more traumatic for large sections of the Scottish people.
>
> Devine and Mitchison (1)

Now *Waverley* marks a change – a sea-change – in world literature because it is itself about change, and changing Scotland, changing both akin to and unlike Europe, constitutes a further context in which both it and its European popularity are to be understood.

Among the changes underway in Scotland between 1745 and 1814 were, in industry, the growth in areas as diverse as lime, coal and kelp, the rise of mechanized milling for lint and linen, and the explosion of the cotton business; in agriculture, the spread of the increasingly profitable cattle and large-scale sheep farming; and in finance, the use of bank notes to a degree unprecedented in Europe. Among the accompanying disruptions were urbanization 'growing more rapidly in Scotland at this time than anywhere else in Europe' (Smout, 1990, 1); population growth, which between 1801 and 1811 was higher than ever before or since; and vast advances in infrastructure and communications – notably the military roads of Wade and Caulfield constructed from the 1720s to the 1760s and the early nineteenth-century bridges of Telford. Among the accompanying traumas were the radical suppression of the clan culture following the Jacobite uprising of 1745, the cruel evictions during the clearances in the Highlands from 1782 on, and severe, war-affected fluctuations in prices often leading to meal riots. Underlying all the above, however, was one further over-riding factor: Scotland, which had joined the United Kingdom in the Union of 1707 was now feeling the full brunt of that change – in increased commercialism, creeping Anglicization and the steady ousting of Scots as a language. Some Scotsmen were beginning to call themselves North Britons and, as David Daiches has nicely pointed out, it was a Scotsman who wrote 'Rule Britannia!' and another who founded the *Encyclopaedia Britannica* (1771). All in all, the great social historian T. C. Smout has written, the Scotland of Scott's lifetime is 'a watershed between one kind of society and another' (Smout and Wood, 1990, 2).

Such a listing of this all-pervading welter of changes may seem unhelpful but the welter is the point. Given the all-pervasiveness of these changes in his native Scotland, there is no need here painfully to reconstruct Scott's connection to them. At Abbotsford, he was little more than a stone's throw from the then booming wool town of Galashiels (and just days after moving in, in May 1812, he forestalled a weavers' riot in the town). At Edinburgh, he was experiencing urban growth day in day out – indeed, born on the College Wynd, moving to George Square in 1776 and writing most of *Waverley* at 39 (North) Castle Street, he lived through and in the emergence of that juxtaposition of Old Town and New which most now understand by Edinburgh.

The listing, however, helps one also to appreciate *which* of these changes interested Scott – and which not – and therefore which are likely to have inspired the emergence of the historical novel. Scott, the list reminds one, is not a George Eliot or Dickens *avant la lettre*: he is not the novelist of Galashiels, nor even of contemporary Edinburgh. His one contemporary novel, *St Ronan's Well* (1824), though very much concerned with change and the new ways men organize time (or it them), is set in the bustling backwater of an emergent spa. Nevertheless, both that novel and its fellows are replete with contemporary references and *obiter dicta* which help one to understand Scott's own understanding of change.

As devotees of Scott's life and fiction will know, Scott, who in *St Ronan's Well* claims to have 'known wheel-road, bridle-way, and footpath for thirty years' (*SR* 1), was fascinated by infrastructure. Be it the military roads, 'broad accesses of the best possible construction' (*HW* 1), welcomed in *The Highland Widow* (1827) or the drove-road, the 'broad green or grey track, which leads across the pathless moor' (*TD* 1) taken in *The Two Drovers* (1827) or even the 'road west-awa' yonder' (*RR* 27), the tobacco trade with America hailed by Bailie Jarvie in *Rob Roy* (1818), Scott could rarely resist a road or route and the possibilities it opened up or closed out. Scott's best-known road is that traipsed from Edinburgh to London by Jeanie Deans as she seeks pardon for her sister in *The Heart of Midlothian* (1818), but it should not be overlooked that Waverley's journeys are, overall, some three times as long as hers. Both he and she trace the map of a newly opened and linked world of which the historical novel will be the cartographer.

Along and beside these new arteries is developing a system which Scott views with equal attention: 'The times have changed in nothing more' – he states in the first sentence of *The Heart of Midlothian* – 'than in the rapid conveyance of intelligence and communication betwixt one part of Scotland and another'. The position and reliability of post-house or post-office plays its part in both *Rob Roy* and *St Ronan's* and the speed or otherwise of the mails is a frequent issue in Scott's work – not least in *Waverley*, where the plot partly hinges on the dispatch, receipt and interception of letters. Such plots are the objective correlative of something which will fascinate the nineteenth-century historical novelist: the possibilities of communication and non-communication in a world increasingly reliant on the former.

Among the mails comes a missive of even greater importance for the genre: the newspaper. Whereas in *Rob Roy*, set in 1715, the protagonist is lucky once to receive 'a printed journal or News-Letter, seldom extending beyond the capital' (*RR* 14), Scott elsewhere remarks on what our chronology details – a new 'mart of news' (*HM* 1) opening up in his day. As early as 1740, Hume had written in his *Treatise* that important news was 'propagated with celerity, heard with avidity, and enquired into with attention and concern'. By 1832, however, in his *Philosophy of History* Hegel goes further:

> In recent times circumstances are totally changed. Our intellectual life is essentially one of construal immediately transforming all events into reports for the mind.

Between these two philosophers and circumscribed by them is the world in and for which the historical novel is written: a world in which, as Scott writes in *Waverley*, 'every mechanic at his six-penny club may nightly learn from twenty contradictory channels the yesterday's news of the capital' (7) – a world of proliferating reports, in which the historical novel will itself become a telling report on reporting.

Though no Balzac, Dickens or Galdós, Scott does also chart the rise of the urban centres to and from which this new intelligence is speeding and in which the people and power increasingly reside. Memorably he evokes the growth of Edinburgh from the 'close-built, high-piled city' of 1707 in *The Heart of Midlothian* (*HM* 8) through the city of 1745 'stretching along the ridgy hill which slopes eastward from the castle' in *Waverley* (191) via the city of 1766 in *Redgauntlet* with the inhabitants choosing 'to imitate some of the conveniences or luxuries of an English dwelling-house, instead of living piled up above each other in flats' (*RG* Letter 5) to the Edinburgh of *Guy Mannering* at the end of the American Wars, when 'the New Town on the north, since so much extended, was then just commenced' (*GM* 36). Now, *Waverley* is emphatically not a novel of urban life. It spends only ten chapters in Edinburgh, two in Carlisle and just one in London (which it touches once more). Fully three quarters of the novel take place in the countryside and almost half in the open air. Nevertheless, the shadow of London lies heavy over its events – not as the 'infernal wen', but as the long arm of central authority.

For of all the changes listed above there is one which grips Scott as man and novelist more – more even than Bonaparte – informing the best of his fiction and prompting in his *Letters of Malachi Malagrowther* (1826) his most emphatic and successful incursion into politics: this is the Union with England and its repercussions, economic, political and cultural. As early as 1806, in introducing the fruits of his ballad-collecting, the *Minstrelsy of the Scottish Border*, Scott had written:

> By such efforts, feeble as they are, I may contribute something to the history of my native country, the peculiar features of whose manners and character are daily melting and dissolving into those of her sister and ally. (*MB*, cxxxi)

By 1826, looking back over the years in which almost all his historical fiction was written, he gives his persona, Malachi Malagrowther, a more disgruntled name and tone:

> I am old, sir, poor, and peevish, and, therefore, I may be wrong; but when I look back on the last fifteen or twenty years, and more especially on the last ten, I think I see my native country of Scotland, if it is yet to be called by a title so discriminative, falling, so far as its national, or rather, perhaps, I ought now to say its *provincial*, interests are concerned, daily into more absolute contempt.
> (*MM* I, 4)

The immediate issue of the *Letters* is the planned suppression of the (economically vital) Scottish bank-notes but Scott seizes the occasion to lament and deplore the suppression of Scottishness at large. And by now he knows at which door the blame is to be laid:

> there has been in England a gradual and progressive system of assuming the management of affairs entirely and exclusively proper to Scotland,

as if we were totally unworthy of having the management of our own concerns. All must centre in London. (*MM* II, 76)

In 1813–15, therefore, Scotland had escaped Bonaparte only to find another *Hannibal ante portas* – a Hannibal who was to have just as much effect on *Waverley* and its European progeny: the Hannibal of empire and centralism with their threat of cultural hegemony.

As early as *The Lay of the Last Minstrel* (1805) Scott had dramatized a sense of cultural demise in the very title of a work. *Waverley*, however, takes the process further, depicting both an ageing bard and the demise of an entire accompanying clan culture. Defeated at Culloden in 1746, proscribed in 1747 and often hounded from their homes into army or emigration, the clans were never to recover. For sure, by no means all the clans were involved in the Forty-five and the seeds of clan decay were sown long before. Nevertheless, the rising can justly be depicted as a swan-song, as precipitating the 'end of the Clan system' (Livingstone, v). When the highlanders are mentioned in Scott's novels set after 1745, as by Darsie in *Redgauntlet*, then the '"broadswords have passed into other hands; the targets are used to cover butter-churns; and the race has sunk, or is fast sinking, from ruffling bullies into tame cheaters"' (*RG* Letter 3). This sense of things ending, of lastness, was to be one of Scott's major cultural legacies. Balzac's first historical novel was originally entitled *The Last Chouan*, Mickiewicz's great Polish epic *Pan Tadeus* (1834) was subtitled 'The Last Feud in Lithuania' and Cooper had anticipated them both with *The Last of the Mohicans* (1826). The historical novel became the genre of irretrievability, of worlds irredeemably going under.

This process, however, offers Scott much more than elegiacs: it is rich in related character and theme. As Scott remarks with hindsight in the preface to *Chronicles of the Canongate* (1827):

The Highlands should furnish you with ample subjects of recollection. You have witnessed the complete change of that primeval country, and have seen a race not far removed from the earliest period of society melted down into the great mass of civilization; and that could not happen without incidents striking in themselves and curious as chapters in the history of the human race. (*CC* Intro.)

Just how ample those subjects would prove is evinced by the Waverley Novels, just how striking, by the history of the genre. In the rough terrain between Union and clan many an historical novel lies waiting.

Scott's complex attitude to the Union is worked out in the space a novelist has for working out such complexities – in the rich casts and occasions of his works. Suffice it to note here that when his characters take sides on the issue, when Deans in the *Heart of Midlothian* rails against the 'nation-wasting and church-sinking abomination of union' (*HM* 12) or when Osbaldistone in *Rob Roy* writes more moderately of the 'national dislike' between the two lands as 'the natural consequence of their existence as separate and rival states' (*RR* 4), the very words 'nation' and 'national' fall readily. The epithet 'national' is especially frequent in Scott, notably in *Waverley* and *Rob Roy*, and is used to characterize not only dress, music and churches, not only peculiarities, characteristics and character, but feeling, hate and freedom also. Now, as historians such as Hobsbawm (1990) remind us, in their modern and basically political sense these concepts are 'historically very young' (18): their use in Scott is among their earliest appearances in high literature. And equally young are the – man-made – realities to which they refer. For nations are almost never preordained but forged: borders are not given but drawn. In other words, 'Nations do not make states and nationalisms but the other way round' (Hobsbawm, 10), and a further mark of the quality and prescience of *Waverley* is that it portrays and analyses the forces so named.

In terms of post-Tönnies sociology, the 'melting down' of clan into United Kingdom is a transition from *Gemeinschaft* to *Gesellschaft*. Elsewhere Scott remarks that 'There are, I believe, more associations common to the inhabitants of a rude and wild than of a well cultivated and fertile country' (*HM* 38). And certainly, the clans of *Waverley* show more allegiance and devotion than the age to which they succumb – an age in which Edward's politically opportunist father holds the constituency of Barterfaith, where the lawyer in the novel hails from the firm of Clippurse and Hookem, and where the '*Diva Pecunia* of the Southron' (333) holds sway.

For the European audience, however, it was not only that the process of melting down was premonitory. The backwardness of the clans had an equal allure. Writing his *Observations on the Present State of the Highlands* in 1806, the Earl of Selkirk put it graphically: 'It must not be forgotten that little more than half a century has passed, since that part of the kingdom was in a state similar to that of England before the Norman conquest'. That is perhaps too graphic: the clans were customarily categorized as feudal – by Montesquieu and repeatedly in *Waverley* by Scott himself. As one of the earliest reviews, in the *Scots Magazine* for July 1814, stated, 'All the feudal habits and ideas, extinct in every other country, reigned here with a sway almost undiminished.' But therefore – the review cannily remarks, anticipating some of his European allure – Scott was also portraying 'in some degree what all Europe was, at the distance of three centuries'.

To the readers of 1814, *Waverley* thus held up a double mirror: the product of a swiftly modernizing country, it reflected the new links and allegiances of modernity; but the product also of a till recently in part backward country, it showed *in nuce* the steps on the path to that modernity.

'It is no accident,' writes Lukács, 'that this new type of novel arose in England' (30). But it didn't: it arose in, and partly because of, the doubly different world of a changing Scotland.

This third, Scottish context thus helps to account for a good deal more of *Waverley*, but even now the accounting is far from over. It still has to be shown why Scott should want to *preserve* these ancient manners, and to preserve them in this way.

4 'These giddy-paced times' and the Age of the Museum

> there have been more changes in this poor nook of yours within the last forty years, than in the great empires of the East for the space of four thousand, for what I know. *St Ronan's Well*, XV

When Scott (1770/1–1832) himself writes of the years through which he lived he repeatedly calls them 'these giddy-paced times': the term occurs in both *The Antiquary*, set in 1805 (*TA* 5), and *St Ronan's Well* set in the 1820s (*SR* 1). And here too Scott is corroborated by contemporaries and modern historians alike: Lord Selkirk writes of 'violent and rapid change' and Smout confirms that 'the pace of change quickened so suddenly' (1969, 230). All these remarks are references to what European historians such as Braudel and Koselleck identify as a central feature of the age and a further cause of the rise of history: not mere change, but rapid, even exponential change. This too is an essential context in which to see *Waverley*, which itself describes change as 'steadily and rapidly progressive' (340).

Just around 1814, Scott's writing is replete with references to the sheer pace of change and sheer speed of loss. In *Paul's Letters*, he records how, to anyone talking in 1815 of events just four years past, the French would reply, ' "*Ah! parlez-moi d'Adam et d'Eve*" ' – 'A retrospective of three or four years,' he comments, 'was like looking back to the fall of man' (*PL* 432). Elsewhere, an interval of just two years seems like an eternity:

> Could the fable of the Seven Sisters have been realized in Paris, what a scene of astonishment would have been prepared for those who, falling asleep in 1813, awakened from their torpor at the present moment! ... The revolution of ages must have appeared to him to have been accomplished within the space of little more than twenty-four months. (*PL* 294–5)

Such precise time-checks will become the hallmark of Scott. Whereas the social novel is marked by 'particularized time and place' (Watt, 22), Scott is the novelist of the particularized *duration*.

One effect of the ongoing transformations he charts was that political stances were forever in flux: these were 'times when universal example sanctioned changes of principle' (*PL* 426). In Paris he records the existence of a *Dictionnaire des Girouettes*, in which those who had turned their coats only once were *not* included. Wavering was part of the age.

A further effect is found by following the motif of the waking sleeper through the literature of the time. The motif is present in 'Thomas the Rhymer', an earlier prose fragment (probably of 1798–9) which Scott later had printed as an appendix to the 1829 General Preface to *Waverley* because it was 'one of the first etchings of the plate' (361). Having visited Scott in 1817 and discussed that tale with him, Washington Irving, however – combining the motif with several from *Waverley* itself – produced not only the first American short-story but also the most memorable exploitation of the topos itself in his *Rip van Winkle* (1819). It is Rip who articulates what was one of the central experiences of the age: 'Every thing's changed – and I'm changed – and I can't tell what's my name, or who I am!'

What does one do when one feels that one is irretrievably losing something cherished and, with it, losing one's bearings in life? After all, as Scott writes in *Guy Mannering*, 'We are not made of wood or stone, and the things which connect themselves with our hearts and habits cannot, like bark of lichen, be rent away without our missing them' (*GM* 6). To this question, social historians and sociologists give two answers.

First, when the familiarities and comforts of continuity are taken away, one creates surrogate invariants: in the terms of recent historiography, one 'invents traditions'. This process, writes Hobsbawm, is likely to 'occur more frequently when a rapid transformation of society weakens or destroys the social patterns' (1983, 4) and it tends to be dated from precisely Scott's period. Indeed, in the establishment of a 'Scottish' tradition – with kilts, distinctive clan tartans and bagpipes, none of which is as ancient as their wearers or players would perhaps like to believe – Scott is often seen as a central figure. One must distinguish here between Scott the writer and Scott the writer as marketed. It may be that, as Trevor-Roper has written, 'the Waverley Novels combined with the Highland regiments to spread the fashion for kilts and tartans throughout Europe' (1983, 28), but in *Waverley* itself Fergus the chieftain correctly wears the trews (89). Nevertheless, his clan, perhaps incorrectly, is given a tartan of its own (178, 197) and when in 1822 George IV made the first state visit to Scotland by a Hanoverian monarch and, in an Edinburgh 'tartanized' for the occasion, donned a tartan of *his* own (no doubt looking a proper Charlie) Scott was the inventive master of the tradition-forging ceremonies.

The second reaction to imminent loss is to salvage the threatened object into a museum. The museum impulse is far, far older than the Napoleonic years, but it was then that – as again enumerated in the chronology – the 'museological explosion' took place and the *temps des musées* began. Many of the museums to which we now make our pilgrimages were opened or initiated in Scott's life-time – the Albertina in Vienna (1776), the Louvre in Paris (1793), the Nationalmuseet in Copenhagen (1807) and the Koninklijk Museum in Antwerp (1810) to mention but a few – and not a few more opened their doors the world over in the very years the *Waverley Novels* first appeared – such as the Madrid Prado in 1819, the London National Gallery in 1824, the Museo Nacional de Historia in Mexico City in 1825 and the Australian Museum in Sydney in 1827. The first national (the Louvre) and the first American university museum (Yale) originate in these years as do both museum classification and preservation techniques. 'The past for the future' – the motto of the first Polish museum – was very much a motto of the age. And in Scotland it had especial force. The Antiquaries' Musaeum was begun in 1782, that of the University by 1784 and the General Register House (the official Scottish archive), begun in 1774, was some twenty years in advance of its English counterpart, Somerset House in London. Such was museomania in Scotland in fact that by 1814 Scottish newspapers even carried advertisements for itinerant museums plying from town to town.

Both in Scotland and elsewhere, but especially in Scotland, this movement went hand in hand with the rise of antiquarianism. In the bleak post-Union present the future very much needed a past, and with the demise of the clans after 1745 a further motive was at hand. Just as the doyen of the early antiquarians, Clerk of Penicuik, 'employed Roman archaeology in Scotland in such a way as to manifest a nationalism that drew its strength from ancient Caledonian resistance to Rome' (Iain Brown, 1987, 35), so Buchan, would-be doyen of the latter half of the century, saw antiquarianism as no 'frivolous employment adapted to the plodding Antiquary only but to the Historian and Patriot' (Iain Brown, 1980, 45). The Antiquarian Society of Scotland was founded in 1780, the Highland Society in 1784, the Celtic Society in 1820, and lesser bodies sprang up the country over, usually with a museum attached. The dusty, rusty and musty had an irresistible lure. Antiquarianism in Scotland was a state of mind, a place of refuge, and a national and nationalist hobby.

To say that Scott had his fingers in the rust and dust would be an understatement. His *Minstrelsy* had put him among the Bishop Percys of Europe, his *Border Antiquities of England and Scotland* (1814) – published only just after *Waverley* – among the Penicuiks. *The Antiquary* is the affectionate persiflage of a leaning of which he was himself an *aficiando*. If one checks the membership lists of antiquarian societies north and south of the border one finds Scott – by dint of the above – almost invariably an honorary member, and an anonymous volume *Tales of an Antiquary* (1828) is inevitably dedicated to him. By the end of 1814, however, Scott was doubly involved in the *temps des musées* also. His Abbotsford has been nicely described as a 'museum for living', in that it not only contains a museum, but also is one, its – now delightfully mellowed – architecture containing both echoes of earlier Scottish buildings and actual pieces of old Edinburgh rescued into the present. *Waverley* too, however, is an act of conservation, rescuing into 1814 'some idea of the ancient manners of which I have witnessed the almost total extinction' (340).

The phrase 'I have witnessed' underscores the difference between that loss and the earlier missing of minstrelsy. Just as Rip must learn to recognize his own village transformed in his twenty-year absence, just as the St Ronan's visitor must learn to differentiate between New Town and Auld, so *Waverley* too is a coming to terms with losses experienced within the space of a lifetime. The more life expectancy rises in an age of change – it was then, depending on class, rising to some 40 to 60 years – the more we have to learn to lose.

The philosopher of the museum culture, Hermann Lübbe, has argued that 'by progressive musealization we compensate for the painful experience of declining familiarity in an age of exponential change' (18). Or, as a more recent historical novelist, Graham Swift, has written in *Out of this World*: 'When you put something on record, when you make a simulacrum of it, you have already partly decided you will lose it'. This too is a context in which Scott's life and work are to be seen. The collecting which is a central part of his work is a response to the losing which is a central part of his life. And for the greatest of these collections *Waverley* is the fitting depository. It is the new simulacrum of the new losses: the historical novel is the verbal museum.

5 Changing Scott

Hath Fiction's stage for Truth's long triumphs room?
The Vision of Don Roderick, LXI

To explain why Scott should create a verbal museum, however, is not to explain why he should create a verbal museum *of this particular kind*. The question arises because of the much-remarked fact that Scott was a highly successful historical poet before ever writing most of *Waverley*. And the question poses itself with all the more insistence when it is considered that this poetry – in particular *The Lay of the Last Minstrel* (1805), *Marmion* (1808), and *The Lady of the Lake* (1810) – had itself treated not only subjects from the Scottish past but also themes similar to those of the novel-to-come: the conflicts between Scottish and English, highland and lowland, centralizing state and coveted neighbour.

One literary-historical reason often given for Scott's abandoning this successful strain (alternately known as martial lay, verse romance, long ballad or epic) is the name of that other poet-son of Scotland: Byron. For critics such as Saintsbury in the late nineteenth century, 'Scott's immediate inducement to turn from verse to prose romance was undoubtedly the popularity of Byron, with his consequent loss of favour'. Given that for Scott, the captain of literature, matters of market were not always inconsequential this has some plausibility. Scott himself later wrote: 'I felt the prudence of giving way before the more forcible and powerful genius of Byron' (*L* VI, 506).

A second argument is connected with the name of Scotland's most celebrated critical son of the time: Francis Jeffrey. Writing on Scott's second lay, *Marmion*, in the *Edinburgh Review* of April 1808 Jeffrey had concluded: 'To write a modern romance of chivalry, seems to be such a phantasy as to build a modern abbey or an English pagoda'. Given that this was the verdict of a long-standing companion of Scott and friend of the Scott household, it is likely also to have had weight.

Chronology reminds us, however, that of themselves such theories do not suffice. After all, Scott began work on *Waverley* some time before Byron's rise to fame, and he wrote several lays well after Jeffrey's remarks, one – *The Lord of the Isles* (1815) – even after finally publishing *Waverley* itself.

Now, it is true that there are in these verse epics anticipations of the locations, plots and foci of the later historical fiction. As Scott's Edinburgh contemporary Sir James Mackintosh saw, the very settings are similar – settings at 'a point where the neighbourhood of the lowlands affords the best contrast of manners; where the scenery affords the noblest subject of description; and where the wild clan is so near to the court, that their robberies can be connected with the romantic adventures of a disguised king, an exiled lord, and a high-born beauty' (82). From the *Lay* on, the feudal 'customs and manners which anciently prevailed' at these spots are depicted with antiquarian care; in *The Lady of the Lake*, the spot is discovered by the device of a traveller coming unawares into the Highlands; and in *Marmion*, though a *Tale of Flodden Field*, the story 'turns on the private adventures of a fictitious character'. In these and other aspects – notably their understanding portrayal of battle-scenes (Ruskin considered the Flodden of *Marmion* the best such scene in all literature) – the lays can be seen as partial rehearsals for the novels.

One cannot, however, quite agree with the several critics who argue that the lays are 'ballads on the point of turning into novels' or that Scott's historical novel is an extended 'ballad in prose'. What these years show is a continuity of effort to depict the Scottish past culminating in a fruitful discontinuity in the literary form employed. The extraordinary gestation of *Waverley* is due to all the self-consciousness, all the unknowing, all the lacking self-confidence of someone breaking radically new ground – but then with increasing panache finding his forte.

For there are essential aspects of *Waverley* which are not prefigured in the lays. First, they lack what it and its successors are justly renowned for: rich characterization, often achieved through conversation, and achieved right across a socially broad cast, thus giving a far different view of causation. *Marmion* has a named cast of some dozen, almost all aristocratic, and even that of *The Lord of the Isles* (1815) – despite its powerful evocation of the field of Bannockburn – is scarcely larger. Further, for all its antiquarian touches, the lay cannot house that detailed thinginess which is the quiddity of Scott's later prose. Nor – not even in *The Vision of Don Roderick* (1811), a four-tableau panorama of the Iberian past – can it do justice to historical continuities, or to *longues durées*. Above all, however, the conflicts the lays portray are set *within* an exclusively feudal past: in *Waverley*, the conflict is *between* a feudal and a more modern society. *Waverley*, in other words, is the appropriate new form for a broader vision, for a Scott who now needs more rooms in his verbal museum than the lay or ballad offers to display all the exhibits he considers necessary for this vision of this past.

It is not that either form – lay/ballad or historical novel – is suited only to the feudal or only to the modern period. The House of the Past, like the House of Fiction, has not one window but a million, and each form will open some windows in either period – the question is only *which* windows and with what resulting view.

The martial lay, Mackintosh argues, 'arose principally from the love of contrast, in the refined and pacific period which preceded the French Revolution' (81). After the unpacific Napoleonic years, however, another view and tone were called for. Scott did later try his hand at a long ballad on Waterloo (again for war charities), but the result is not happy. As one wag had it: 'On Waterloo's ensanguined plain/ Full many a gallant man was slain/ But none by sabre or by shot/ Fell half as flat as Walter Scott'. In his own study of these years, *War and Peace*, Tolstoy argues that the epic 'is meaningless for our epoch' (III, 2, xix) and Scott seems to have moved in that direction, writing to Heber in 1831 that modern epics 'present us with heroes when we would rather have a display of real men and manners' (*L* XII, 284). *Paul's Letters* and '1814' are not least the works of a writer struggling to come to terms with modern warfare, but it is in *Waverley*, at Prestonpans, that this new window is first pushed open.

In literary history Scott is thus, as Carlyle saw, 'the first to see that the day of the epic chivalric romance was declining'. Or, as his German admirer and emulator Alexis wrote: 'The noble Tory put courtly verse to flight once and for all'. His progression from lay and ballad to historical novel was to set a pattern for European writers right up to Fontane in the 1860s and 1870s. The year 1814 thus marks the transition from one literary mode of envisaging the past to another, marks the emergence of Scott as, in Balzac's words, *ce trouvère moderne*, this modern troubadour.

This is not to belittle the lays: they can still grip, intrigue and delight – in the thrust of their verse, in their occasional *sententiae*, in their elegiac sense of pastness and in their resonant evocations of Scottish landscapes from Edinburgh across the highland line to the Cuillins on Skye. But neither is it to deny that *Waverley* is one of those great harvest-homes in which a writer (and a generation of successors) for the first time find their element.

Taken together, the above five contexts – European, intellectual, Scottish, socio-temporal and literary-historical – explain a good deal of the making of *Waverley*. A sociology of the historical novel which deserved the name would have to take at least all five into account. Lukács is embarrassingly vague and wrong on Scott's Scottishness. Even Scottish writers such as Daiches and MacQueen tend to stress the intellectual side of the Scottish inheritance. Perhaps the best pithy understanding of the rise of the genre is to be found in Fleishman:

> As far as it is possible to speak of the social determination of literary phenomena, the rise of the historical novel may be described as the outcome of the age of nationalism, industrialization, and revolution: the age when the European peoples came to consciousness of and vigorously asserted their historical continuity and identity; the century when widening commerce, population shifts and factory organization created a new pattern of day-to-day life and consequent nostalgia for the old; the time when the French Revolution and its successors precipitated what we have come to call the modern world. (17)

If one adds to this the factors of infrastructure, community, exponential change, the simultaneity of the non-simultaneous and the museum culture as suggested above – and recalls the Scottish aspect in each of them – then one has perhaps come nearer to an understanding of why *Waverley* could be written.

6 Scott, the great coaginator

> rain forced me into the Antiquarian Museum. Lounged there until a meeting of the Oil Gas Committee ... *Journal*, 19.ii.1827

And yet, however influential the above contexts, they cannot even together be explanation enough. For – to paraphrase Sartre – Scott may be a child of these years and movements, but not every child of these movements and years is Scott. No account of *Waverley* can be adequate without a consideration of salient factors in Scott's personal biography – as this Scott born in this family, trained to this profession, having these habits of mind, holding these persuasions and indulging these predilections.

Like the protagonists of many of his novels, Scott came from an ancient house, or rather from two – the Scotts and the Rutherfords being both Border families of long-standing, the former with a lineage not only of sheep-farmers but of reivers and Wardens, who feature in some of Scott's early balladry. More importantly, however, the family had itself been divided in the Forty-five. On the fly-leaf of his own copy of the *Genuine Memoirs of John Murray, Esq.* (1747) – Murray being a Secretary to the Young Pretender during the Forty-five, who then turned King's evidence – Scott has written a family anecdote:

> 'What has brought you here?' said my grandfather, who was a bold determined man – 'We are come to make you happy' said the unfortunate Secretary – 'You are come to get yourself hanged' retorted the other. There the debate ended. It would have been more creditable for the Secretary's memory had this prediction been accomplished. My father and one of his brothers, then very young, were on their way to join the Prince but were fetched back by my grandfather.

The motto of *Waverley* – 'Under which King, Benzonian? speak, or die!' – could thus, briefly, have been that of the Scotts.

Though Edinburgh-born, Scott was in key ways Borders-bred. The importance of this is evident in the introduction to his *Border Antiquities of England and Scotland* (1814), published just a few months after *Waverley*. Here Scott remarks that 'The frontier regions of most great kingdoms, while they retain that character, are unavoidably deficient in subjects for the antiquary', but that

> The case becomes different, however, when, losing by conquest or by union their character as a frontier, scenes once the theatre of constant battle, inroad, defence, and retaliation, have been for two hundred years converted into the abode of peace and tranquillity. (*BA* iii)

It was in this evocative context of present peace and past ravage that Scott spent periods of youth, here that he first collected ballads, here that he first indulged his antiquarianism. Sir Herbert Grierson argues that this experience is the 'tap-root of Scott's later work' (72) and *Waverley* itself is a novel very much about borders, about the enmities and prejudices that surround them and about the value of sensitive border-crossing.

Scott was abroad in the Borders not only as a pedestrian antiquary, but also as Sheriff-Depute of Selkirkshire. The son of an Edinburgh Writer to the Signet, Scott was by training and profession a man of the law and (unlike his successor R.L. Stevenson) a well-versed and well-regarded practitioner (though never as financially successful as, say, Boswell). This experience too left its firm imprint on his writing: not only did Scotland's commodious legal vacations give him leisure for his many other pursuits – Cockburn wrote in 1836 that 'It is this abdication from legal business which has given Scotland the greatest part of her literature that has adorned her' – but in an age when written history took on the quality of a forensic inquiry, he was able to devote a lawyer's weighing mind to the past. Lawyers come off badly in *Waverley* as elsewhere in Scott, but the trial scene in which the protagonist's actions are subject to diverse interpretations will become a topos of the European genre, and the genre's early commitment if not to lawyers then to the rule of (humane) law starts here too.

This combination of the literary and the worldly, the past and the present is a hallmark of Scott. Hazlitt's jibe that 'His is a mind brooding over antiquity – scorning "the present ignorant time" ' (Hayden, 279) is inadequate to a man who by 1814 not only held or had held several public appointments in law, but was partner in a publishing business, co-founder of a periodical, Quartermaster of the Light Dragoons and member of numerous societies. As his Abbotsford library, where Jacobite tracts jostle with studies of canal and railway developments, as Abbotsford itself, part imitation castle and yet lit by gas, so Scott too was very much of the modern world – at times too much for his own good. Not least, he was himself not averse to the *Diva Pecunia* (not for its own sake but for what it gave him in terms of land, library and lairdly living) and was so involved with his publishing and printing co-partners that their crash in 1825–6 left him also – of whom Stendhal had written to the French *Députés* in 1820 that he had already acquired by his work riches greater than those of any French writer ever – well-nigh penniless. 'Involved', however, is too pale a word for the intricate maze of bills, counter-bills, advances on anticipated profit and mutual loans which linked Scott to his partners; and 'penniless' is too mild an expression for the reality of Scott's bankruptcy – to the tune of some £127,000 (millions in today's terms). It may not have benefited Scott's writing to feel so often the pinch of his other activities, but it certainly enriched it to be so full of world. If in *Waverley* Scott can dramatize so well the fate of human beings torn between old and new it was not least because he himself felt the dual pull.

This holds true even for Scott's politics, which also leave a dual mark on *Waverley*. In *Malachi Malagrowther*, Scott describes himself as a 'pretty stanch [*sic*] Tory' (*MM* III, 4) and both before and after gave ample evidence in support: he was agin the French Revolution, interpreted the Galashiels incident of 1812 as harbinger of an English *jacquerie*, defended the Peterloo massacre, and in his last years opposed the Reform Bill of 1832. *Paul's Letters* contain several Burkean references to the danger of 'modern political legerdemain' (*PL* 225) and to the value of 'persevering steadiness' (*PL* 449), especially in the monarchy and landed aristocracy. In both *Waverley* and many other of his novels the plot finally confirms a threatened landed gentry in its estates. Like Burke, however, Scott was in favour of temperate amelioration, of some judicious polishing of the family heirlooms. In the dire economic climate of 1819, he instituted a scheme of public works for the needy around Abbotsford and advocated popular education. Cockburn even recalls him welcoming the 1830 revolution in France, exclaiming, 'Confound these French Ministers! I can't forgive them for making a Jacobin of an old Tory like me' (436). Above all, however, Scott was rarely testy, never crusty and was the best of social mixers. In 1832, newspapers across the political spectrum united with the *Caledonian Mercury* in hailing him as 'a liberal-minded man in the best sense of the term and wholly uninfected with that type of acrimony which has been so largely infused both into the politics and literature of our time' – and this broad generosity of sympathy comes through in *Waverley* in the form of a rich cast and balanced appraisals. For all his politics, therefore, Scott democratizes the novel form (an insight now attributed to Lukács but in fact commonplace a hundred years earlier). As Buchan nicely puts it, Scott had little time for the Brotherhood of Man, but in practice regarded all men as brothers (48).

And nowhere is Scott's dualism more evident than in his attitude to Jacobitism. In a renowned letter of 13 July 1813, he writes:

> I am very glad I did not live in 1745 for although as a lawyer I could not have pleaded Charles's right and as a clergyman I could not have prayed for him yet as a soldier I would I am sure against the convictions of my better reason have fought for him even to the bottom of the gallows. (*L* III, 302)

Waverley is the novel in which he is able vicariously to live out both sides of this divided political self.

Finally, such cheek-by-jowl oppositions held in harmony are a mark not only of Scott's life and politics but of his literary mode. The Romantic imagination was described by Coleridge as the 'coaginative faculty' and Scott was in high degree a coaginator. His oeuvre has been nicely characterized by Duncan Forbes as a 'unique blend of sociology and romance, of philosophical history and the novelist's living world of individuals' (35). In terms of literary schools, it was he who, in *Waverley* and thereafter, carried the Enlightenment on into Romanticism and then – via antiquarianism – further forward into European realism.

And so one could go on: the combination of diligent father and artistic mother, the double blessing of an interrupted education and the chance to follow a personal bent, the famous talent for mimicry, the prehensile memory – 'wax to receive and granite to retain' (Buchan, 33) – the gifts of the *raconteur*, the sheer energy to create, the pure strength of a hand schooled in years of legal copy-writing, and all this in 1814 in a man very much on song ... But as Th. Mann wrote in *Lotte in Weimar* (1935), his own historical novel about Scott's great contemporary, Goethe, there can be no full documentation of the cross-fertilizations across the centuries and years that go to make up a writer.

Suffice it to say that in June 1814, when the final two volumes of the novel were written within four weeks – written on Edinburgh evenings by a man who spent six hours a day five days a week working at Court – that energetic hand mesmerized a young advocate in digs across Castle Street: 'it fascinates my eye – it never stops – page after page is finished and thrown down on that heap of MS., and still it goes on unwearied – and so it will be till candles are brought in, and God knows how long after that'. The great coaginator was doing his final bit for the making of *Waverley*.

Chapter 2

Waverley as story

7 New journeys, new plot

The end of uncertainty is the death of interest; and hence it happens that no one now reads novels

The Heart of Midlothian, XIV

The central device, and one of the central metaphors, of *Waverley* is a journey undertaken shortly before the 1745 Uprising by young Edward Waverley – his head full of the romance journeys of yore – followed by a series of further journeys he undertakes both later that year and in 1746. As a metaphor, however, the journey is at least as old as the romance quest tradition in Edward's mind; and as a device it lends itself easily to lax, sequential structure. If, therefore, as the reviewer in the *Scots Magazine* of July 1814 saw, 'The thread which holds the story together is formed by the adventures of a young man, whom family connections and a romantic spirit lead to explore these almost unknown regions', it is worth asking how taut a thread it here is and whether it is made up of any new strands.

The question as to the quality of Scott's plotting has divided critics from the first. In the *Edinburgh Review* of November 1814, Jeffrey wrote that *Waverley* was 'not very skilfully adjusted', whereas the *Monthly Review* of that same month praised 'a chain of circumstances which are very ingeniously and naturally combined by the author'. In an anonymous self-review of 1817 Scott himself sided with Jeffrey, stating that his first novels were 'so slightly constructed as to remind us of a showman's thread with which he draws up his pictures' (Williams, 239), but the debate has not ceased to produce extreme stances – from, say, A. N. Wilson's praise of *Waverley*'s 'splendidly well-organized plot' (48) to E. M. Forster's round declaration on Scott in *Aspects of the Novel* (1927): 'He cannot construct'. It is doubly important, therefore, to grasp how often Edward travels, where, why, with whom in accompaniment, with what in his luggage, with which encounters and to what ultimate end – not only because this is the thread of the novel, but also because these journeys and sojourns are the way into *Waverley*'s plot structure, into its relationship with romance and hence into the debate on its originality and quality.

Even the novel's first book, not renowned for its action, sends young Edward out on three distinct journeys. Early in 1745 (or, some maintain, as early as late 1744), he leaves the family estate of Waverley-Honour in Hampshire, accompanied and followed by a small group of family retainers, to take up an army commission on the east coast of Angusshire. Soon wearying of military tedium, however, he takes a furlough in early summer to visit the Baron of Bradwardine, an antiquarian and old Jacobite acquaintance of his Tory uncle living with his nubile daughter Rose at Tully-Veolan, an estate and village just south of the highland line. Here, some six weeks later, a raid by highland cattle thieves and its subsequent reconciliation afford him an opportunity to make a third journey on into the Highlands themselves, where, after a night's stay in the cave of the robber Donald Bean Lean and his band, he moves on to visit – and, it transpires, stay for a further month or so in – the castle at Glennaquoich, centre of the declining but still martial clan of the Mac-Ivors under their young Jacobite chieftain Fergus and his alluring sister Flora.

These journeys and visits set up four encounters essential alike to the genre and to Scott's late-Enlightenment and Napoleonic Age vision of society. Most obviously, they are the rites of passage of an *ingénu* into the world of affairs, not least of love affairs – rites in which a romance vision of life can receive a douche of realism. They are equally a first brush with the military. And they are further the first sojourn of an Englishman in recently annexed Scotland – and thus in and among the realities of centralization, nationalism and national prejudices. Above all, however, they are journeys to the edge of lowland civilization and then over the edge into a different stage of society – journeys, that is, into an awareness of that central issue in late-Enlightenment history and sociology: the simultaneity of the non-simultaneous. And therefore, they are journeys which allow Waverley to fulfil his novel birthright and to sway in allegiance not just between two women, but between two visions of life, two sides, two politics, two cultures, two futures.

The leisurely pace of the first volume with these three pacific journeys is replaced in volume II by fully seven journeys, each more fraught or violent than its predecessor, each demanding brief analysis, and each soon to have its case-history of emulation and extrapolation in European historical fiction. From Glennaquoich, Edward is taken by Fergus on a stag-hunt, in which not only the Mac-Ivor retainers but several other clans participate, during which Fergus confers with his fellow chieftains and on which Edward is saved only by Fergus from losing his life in a stampede of desperate animals.

This stampede is a symbol of how Waverley is being overrun by events beyond his ken and control. For, as the chieftains' deliberations suggest, things are afoot. From now on it is clear that *Waverley* has done what so many a successful historical novel has subsequently also done – launched its protagonist, unknowing, into the thick of significant past events, in this case events which the reviewers of 1814 still saw as a period 'peculiarly critical', as a 'period to which no Briton can look back without the strongest emotions', as 'that memorable year in our annals, 1745'. Thus the hunt inaugurates also what will become a major theme in historical fiction, the theme of the two lives of any human being – the unknowing, but ostensibly free life we live forwards and the knowing but ever more determined life we later understand backwards. To Edward, the stag-hunt is a stag-hunt: to Scott, Fergus and the alert reader, it is the beginning of the Forty-five.

But what is it to Edward's military commanders or to the authorities in the Lowlands? This issue of interpretation dominates Edward's next two moves. For whereas the journey to Tully-Veolan has been sanctioned leave, the further journeys have not. And not only is his commander unaware of Edward's harmless intentions, but Edward is unaware that his family troop has been manipulated into mutiny. Indeed, his commander, sensing straws in the wind, has summoned him back to camp, but neither this letter nor a successor has reached its addressee. On returning to Glennaquoich after some five days spent recuperating from his injuries, Edward thus opens his mail to find himself cashiered. And on hastening down into the Lowlands to clear his name he finds himself arrested in the village of Cairnvreckan and confronted with even more: not only the above, but a Catholic history by his tutor foisted on him as he left home and a rebellious poem by Flora now found in his pocket – all are now paraded and interpreted in his disfavour. Edward wishes to confirm his alignment with Hanover, but his accusers arraign him with Jacobitism.

In his early review Jeffrey writes of Edward losing his commission 'in consequence of some misunderstandings which it is unnecessary to detail'. Both the thrust of *Waverley*'s themes and the development of the genre, however, suggest that more is at stake. Scott's plotting is here the objective correlative of the emergent age of communication sketched in above. Both society and novel resemble a Chinese-box in which characters inhabiting different boxes can still live in mutual unawareness and mutual misinterpretation. Many an historical novel protagonist will be able, like Edward, to look back on 'the mazes of the labyrinth, in which he had been engaged' (309). (Complicated and deepened, this structure will eventually become the philosophy of history in Tolstoy's *War and Peace*.) And many will encounter 'men of ready and acute talent' who, like the Cairnvreckan magistrate Major Melville and the local minister Mr Morton, nevertheless arrive at 'a great discrepancy in their respective deductions from admitted premises' (161–2). Indeed, the cross-examination scene of II, 8, in which Edward's actions are interpreted with the utmost uncharitableness by the one and with benignness by the other will become a generic topos. In an age increasingly reliant on unreliable information, an age when history itself is said to have become a 'forensic process', Scott is the first of many historical novelists to bring the fickleness of historical interpretation to the fore.

Edward's journey to the Lowlands is, however, not least

just that. As he rides into Cairnvreckan to find the village aghast at rumours of a rising, the smith furbishing arms despite the Sabbath, tempers frayed, nerves on edge and himself suspected of being Secretary Murray or even the Chevalier, he and the reader are led to see the very different temper of the Lowlands as regards matters of legitimacy, civil order and religion. This scene at the smithy is in *Waverley* the first of several episodes, and in the genre the first of countless, which show the social side of war, military events 'coming home' to the common populace.

Soon, however, they are to come home to Edward himself. For in the space of the final fourteen chapters of volume II, he is first escorted off towards captivity in Carlisle under the harsh eye of a fanatical Cameronian, Gifted Gilfillan, then rescued and wafted into hiding for a week – at, we later learn, the instigation of Rose – then led via the Jacobite garrison of Doune to Edinburgh, where he meets and pledges himself to the Chevalier, and then involved in the first battle of the rebellion, the rout of an English army at nearby Prestonpans.

These four marches precipitate Edward into two of the now canonical scenes of the genre: the meeting of protagonist and leader-figure, and the experience of a greenhorn or rank civilian on a field of battle. The importance of the one is perhaps best adumbrated as a corrective to any Great Man view of the past, that of the other as the place from which the war novel starts. Above all, however, Edward has by now not just wavered, but plumped for Stuart rather than Hanover.

Yet, equally essential to the plot are three other encounters Edward has as events hurtle him on: just before Prestonpans, he stumbles across the dying Houghton, one of his family retainers mortally wounded in a skirmish with the insurgents he is now sided with; both before and during the battle, he spots his former commander, Colonel G—, who then also dies with reproach in his glance; and at the battle's end, he himself rescues from death and makes prisoner a certain Captain Talbot, who, it transpires, has come to Scotland in search of him. Each meeting compels him to confront his disloyalty and to reflect both on the causes between which he is wavering and on the effects of wavering itself: ' "O, indolence and indecision of mind! if not in yourselves vices, to how much exquisite misery do you prepare the way!" ' (219).

The *Monthly Review* wrote that 'from this point in the story, the remaining adventures of the hero are merely so many incidents subservient to a more spirited and accurate narrative of the military operations of the Pretender'. And it is certainly true that as the third volume opens Edward returns with the Chevalier to Edinburgh, stays there with him until early November, and then, in an army of some 6,000, begins the march into England via Carlisle and through Lancashire to Derby, where in early December the decision is taken to turn back. Following a skirmish at Clifton on 18 December, however, Edward is separated from the insurgents and never sees army or Prince again – and yet has still to cover more than half the distance he travels in the novel.

The march south is an early example of an historical novel taking time to portray the realities not just of warfare, but of the convictions and motives behind it – notably in the character of Fergus. As such it leads Edward to doubt the wisdom of the course he has plumped for, the retreat beaten by the Jacobites running parallel to the countermarch of the romantic impulses in his mind.

Having hidden in a secluded farmhouse near Ullswater until the end of January, Edward learns in the press of the death of his father and of a threat to his uncle and so again journeys in an attempt to clear the family name, this time travelling incognito to London on a three-week coach journey. Learning, however, from Talbot that he is *persona non grata* in the capital, he returns to Scotland by horse to petition for Rose's hand, reaching the Borders in early April 1746 and travelling on via Edinburgh and Perth to Tully-Veolan – only to find government troops quartered near the village, the house sacked and of the Bradwardines no trace.

The second of these journeys casts Edward in a role which will become part of the stock-in-trade of the genre: the Rip van Winkle figure returning to a familiar spot and tracing the effect of events or of the passage of time both on it and him.

'Now, how changed, how saddened, yet how elevated was his character, within the course of a very few months! Danger and misfortune are rapid, though severe teachers' (296). The earlier journey, however, back to the centre to seek clemency, traces out the new political realities, which will henceforth dominate both plot and country.

When it turns out that the Baron is not dead but hiding in a nearby cave and that Rose also is safe, the longest journey of all is mooted – to exile in France – and is forestalled only when Talbot procures a pardon for both Baron and Edward. Instead, after a week wooing Rose, Edward hastens to Carlisle, where he witnesses the moving final moments of the trial in which Fergus and his faithful clansman Evan Dhu are sentenced to death, having interviews with both Fergus and Flora before the former's execution. Thereafter, he travels to Waverley-Honour to arrange the marriage and to London to gain his pardon, before returning to Scotland some two months later to claim his bride and settle on the now pacified highland line, in a Tully-Veolan restored to its former glory by Talbot's good offices, just months after the final battle on British soil and with the final fate of the Chevalier still undecided.

Within a year and a half, Edward has thus travelled outwardly in excess of 2,000 miles and inwardly the distance between indecisiveness and resolution: his final journeys both confront him with the consequences of rebellion and express his own conclusion and reconciliation.

The overall structure of *Waverley* will be assessed below, but even so straightforward a re-tracing of its plot makes several things clear – a first being that Edward's journey does have affinities with the romance quests under way in his mind. The sequential adventure, the successful quest leading through perilous journey (*agon*) and crucial struggle (*pathos*) to a final elevation of the hero (*anagnorisis*), the dual heroines, the bride as reward at the journey's end and the well-nigh miraculous house-warming presided over by an avuncular figure – all these are familiar elements of romance as analysed by Northrop Frye in *The Anatomy of Criticism*.

Equally clear, however, is that between *Waverley* and

romance plots there are also distinct differences. By and large, the marvellous is lacking: Scott justly describes his narrative as not 'a flying chariot drawn by hyppogriffs, or moved by enchantment' but a 'humble English post-chaise, drawn upon four wheels, and keeping his majesty's highway' (24). Moreover, Edward is not a 'central character who never develops' (Frye, 1957, 186) – and one of the main things he learns in developing is to distrust the distorting prism of the romance vision. In an article on 'Romance' in the *Encyclopaedia Britannica* of 1826 – an article he agreed to write in 1814 – Scott defines romance as 'a fictitious narrative in prose or verse; the interest of which turns upon marvellous and uncommon incidents' and the novel as 'a fictitious narrative, differing from the romance, because accommodated to the ordinary train of human events, and to the modern state of society'. In these terms, *Waverley* is not only a novel, but a novel whose protagonist has to make that accommodation. It is a nice characterization of this congruity of plot and theme when, in his fuller study of romance, *The Secular Scripture* – which makes repeated reference to *Waverley* – Frye sites Scott 'on the boundary of serious fiction and romance' (42).

The ease with which *Waverley* traces and traverses that boundary is due to an important feature of its journeys. When at the novel's end Scott remarks, 'Our journey is now finished, gentle reader' (339) he is pointing out that family retainers were not Edward's only travelling companions: *Waverley* is the first of those historical novels in which an unknowing traveller is sent out to reconnoitre accompanied and commented on by a knowing author at his side. When Edward errs over the border into romance, Scott is there to map and re-direct his straying ways.

The essential – and innovatory – aspect of Edward's wanderings, however, is their unerringly apt reconnoitring of a multi-dimensional past. Edward's geographical journey is in two senses also a time-journey: it leads the reader back into that foreign country which is the past of 1745, but it also leads both the reader and Edward into that further foreign country which is the yet more backward present of a still feudal highland culture. In wandering from age to age, stage to stage and camp to camp, the plot is the new structure of a new action – the magnificently appropriate form for experience and adjudication of times past.

What makes *Waverley* so important a reconnaissance, however, is the sheer range of experience it opens up. In the nineteenth century it was common to contrast Scott's breadth with the narrowness of Fielding or of the continental *Individualroman*. Carlyle wrote admiringly of Scott's 'wider sweep' (Hayden, 361), Ruskin praised his 'larger view of human life' (Hayden, 525), and Edward's wanderings and encounters are such that *Waverley* has, with *some* justification, been called not only the first historical novel, but also the first political, the first nationalist and the first regional novel – with some claim also to being the first meta-historical novel.

If one needs any further evidence for the potential of Scott's plot one has only to cast an eye to the European mainland. For, as hinted above, not the least remarkable feature of Edward's journey is that it is soon re-traced by many a continental counterpart, and re-traced doggedly. To have mastered the plot of *Waverley* is to have the Baedeker to the early historical novel at hand.

Finally, all this means that the image of Scott the slipshod writer must in the case of *Waverley* (and not only of *Waverley*) be revised. Balzac believed that *Kenilworth* was Scott's best plot, but there is a strong case for agreeing with Carlyle that 'On the whole, contrasting *Waverley*, which was carefully written, with most of its followers which were written extempore, one may regret the extempore method' (Hayden, 365) – except that, given the quality of the product, the matter of how fast Scott wrote is here, though interesting, immaterial. *Waverley*, the distillation of key experiences of the early nineteenth century, had demonstrably been in Scott's mind for at least some years and the rich fittingness of its plot reminds one that it is not only when writing that a writer writes.

8 New encounters, new cast

'I am sure I will undertake the cause of any poor man with pleasure, and bestow upon it as much pains as if it were a duke's.'

Redgauntlet, Letter XIII

If plot is the structure of an action, cast is the exploration of its human possibilities. The cast of *Waverley* is a further innovation, so evolved as to make Edward's journeys rich in thematic encounter and so deployed as to underpin Scott's reading of the Forty-five.

The essential innovation in this cast, from which several others flow, is its sheer size. It numbers some sixty-five named characters who tread the boards of the novel, some twenty-five further named characters who stay in the wings, a further thirty-odd who appear but are not named, and many groups – from the shed 'crowded with persons' at Cairnvreckan (150), through the 'about a hundred Highlanders, in complete dress and arms' training at Glennaquoich (94) to the 'mixed and wavering multitude' of the Jacobites approaching Prestonpans (213). Numbers are not everything here, but it is noteworthy that the first of these figures is some five times as high as in Maria Edgeworth's *Castle Rackrent* (1800), fully twice as many as in Jane Austen's *Sense and Sensibility* (1811), and substantially in excess both of many novels of Balzac and of all *Waverley*'s immediate successors in Europe.

Surveying this array, the *Monthly Review* wrote that 'almost every variety of station and interest, such as it existed at the period under review, is successively brought before the mind of the reader in colours vivid and original'. An analysis of the cast, however, suggests that this judgement is truer of station than of interest.

Of the main cast, some fifteen are members of the landed classes, some four or five are officers and some ten from the professions, the remaining half being from the lower ranks in civilian life or army. If one adds that the landed classes are represented both in England (the Waverleys and Talbots) and in Scotland on both sides of the highland line (the Mac-Ivors, the Bradwardines and the several lairds around Tully-Veolan);

that the professions range from clergyman (Mr Morton, Mr Rubrick), through tutor (Mr Pembroke) to bookseller and clan bard; that the lower classes are portrayed in Highlands, Lowlands and England and range from soldiery, English and Scottish, through farmer, housewife, smith, tailor, butler, attendants (male and female) and servants, to robber and fool; and that the unnamed characters stretch from clan leach to Edinburgh's notorious 'Circes of the High Street' (213) – then one can see that Scott has indeed mustered a rich roll-call of 1745 society.

When it comes to the interests involved, however, the roll-call has some absentees. One cannot accuse Scott of ignoring the Hanoverian viewpoint: that would be to overlook Edward's wavering and the two English Colonels, G— and Talbot. Nor can one quite accuse him here of what Murray Pittock has accused him in general – of 'making the Jacobite cause stand for Scottish national feeling as a whole' (85): that would be to ignore the scenes in Cairnvreckan and the figures of Major Melville and Gilfillan. And certainly highland Jacobitism is itself well represented in Fergus, Flora and Evan Dhu. Nevertheless, it remains the case that of the main cast only a third are English, that of the remaining Scots only seven are definitely non-Jacobite and that of the highlanders none is non-Jacobite at all. It is a revealing deployment of cast in a story of a failed rising when the three groups most responsible for the rising's failure are the three least represented.

For all this restriction, however, Scott's casting of the rebellion remains broad, and its breadth allows Edward to explore not only the pros and cons of rebellion but a wealth of human ramifications. In his verse epics Scott's preferred method of exploring theme had been through character contrast, and here too one finds the contrasting pairs: Fergus–Talbot, Flora–Rose, Sir Everard–Richard, and Bradwardine–Fergus, and less prominently Richard–Evan Dhu, Morton–Gilfillan and Mucklewrath–Jopson. As many critics have noted, however, the wider scope of the novel allows Scott to form here clusters of characters, who from their several viewpoints illuminate issues as varied as rebellion, honour, courage, nationalism, cultural tolerance, romance, response to change, historiography and life as self-narration. Character tends to recede before issue and it is hence in terms of the latter that the central sections of this study are structured.

None of this is to imply, however, that the cast of *Waverley* is a colourless construct. On the contrary, from the earliest reviews, readers have noted both the vivacity of the cast and some of the means by which this is achieved. The *Scourge* spoke of an 'admirable delineation of native scenery and manners' and the *Monthly Review* of characters 'drawn not only with fidelity but with considerable humour', while the *British Critic* argued that 'The livelier scenes which are displayed in the course of the tale are of the most amusing species, because they flow so naturally from the personages before us, that the characters, not the author appear to speak.' Certainly, these three aspects – the affectionate humour and the use of dialogue, both applied to a largely Scottish context – are major contributions to Scott's success here. Equally important is the novel's style – partaking, Scott himself concedes, 'of what the scholars call the periphrastic and ambagitory, and the vulgar the circumbendibus' (116) – which allows for many an exposition *en route*. And Scott revels in the wryly eloquent name, not only for his protagonist and dual heroines, but for characters as varied as the Waverley lawyer Mr Clippurse, Mr Pembroke's desired publisher Jonathan Grubbet, the irascible Cairnvreckan smith John Mucklewrath, the over-inquisitive Mrs Nosebag, prying companion on Edward's incognito journey south, the Tully-Veolan clergyman Mr Rubrick, the French officer M. de Beaujeu and the English officer Major Whacker.

Although such techniques are a continuation of the British novel tradition from Fielding through Richardson and Smollett to Maria Edgeworth, the areas and quality of their application here give them two further novelties. There had been novels set in the Scottish past before – notably those of Jane Porter – but this large Scottish cast nevertheless amounts to what the *Monthly Review* called 'so wide a field of original delineation', and what some reviewers thought a risk on the English book-market. Equally, many reviewers commented on how Scott's techniques and sympathy are applied throughout his cast list, Jeffrey even claiming:

> The lower scenes ... though to some fastidious readers they may appear coarse and disgusting, are painted with a force and a truth to nature, which equally bespeak the powers of the artist, and are incomparably superior to anything of the sort which has been offered to the publick for the last sixty years.

In human and literary terms this is a rich harvest in felt life. In literary-historical terms it is a major advance towards the novel of social panorama. In sociological and historiographic terms it is a recognition of the role played by 'lay actors', a decisive step towards social rather than 'drum and trumpet' history. In *Waverley*, cast is more than protagonists and mutes: it is a well-fledged ensemble fully engaged.

So what of the work's nominal protagonist, Edward, and its would-be protagonist, the Chevalier? Consideration of them can justly be left till last. For, as the *Monthly Review* saw, 'The Pretender himself, notwithstanding his royal descent, must be classed among the secondary characters of the piece.' Though casting a long shadow from the novel's margins, he actually appears in only five of its chapters. *Waverley* is the first of many historical novels where nominal rank no longer ensures prominence in cast and where leader and led thus tend to exchange briefs, the former emerging as reliant on the latter: Scott himself was to write in an important review of the *Culloden Papers* in 1816 that, after Derby, the Prince 'from being the leader of his little host, became in appearance, as he was in reality, their reluctant follower' (*CP* 285). As Balzac (who renamed his own historical novel from *The Gars* to *The Chouans*) nicely remarked, Scott *'n'a jamais intitulé l'un de ses ouvrages "Le Prétendant", mais "Waverley"'*.

This is not, however, to imply that Edward is the one to upstage the ensemble: the *Quarterly Review* anticipated countless readers in commenting that 'Waverley, who gives his name to the story, is far from being its hero.' It is a fitting final tribute to the breadth and vibrancy of Scott's cast, and a pointer to its greatest innovation, that not even Edward –

who appears not just in a mere five, but in all but three of the chapters – can steal the show.

9 The hero as intermediary

'the facility with which I have, in moments of indolence, suffered my motions to be directed by any person who chanced to be near me, instead of taking the labour of thinking or deciding for myself'

Redgauntlet, III

From the first, Edward Waverley has had a bad press, eclipsed by the novel to which he gives his name. And now that he and his successors are even ensconced in encyclopaedias of poetics as 'Waverley heroes', he might seem beyond redemption. There has, however, been a movement to have his case reviewed and it is now worth asking whether Waverley actually is a 'Waverley hero'.

In 1821, in a famous series of *Letters to Richard Heber* designed to show that Scott was the author of the still anonymous Waverley Novels, J. L. Adolphus described Edward (and his ilk) as

> a hero, who, from the beginning to the end of his history, is scarcely ever left upon his own hands, but appears almost always in the situation of pupil, guest, patient, protégé or prisoner; engaged in a quarrel from which he is unconsciously extricated; half duped and half seduced into rebellion; ineffectually repenting; snatched away by accident from his sinking party; by accident preserved from justice; and restored by the exertions of his friends to safety, fortune and happiness.
>
> (Hayden, 210)

This telling résumé of Scott's plotting soon found an echo on the Continent, where in an important essay, 'The Romances of Walter Scott' (1823), Alexis depicts Scott's heroes as 'amiable nonentities' and their character as an 'extended negative'. At home, many an early reader would have agreed with Frances Lady Shelley and Elizabeth Grant of Rothiemurchus, whose diaries and memoirs dismiss Edward as 'for the most part insipid' and even 'contemptible'. And such views have continued into our century, Lukács seeing the Scott protagonist as a 'more or less mediocre, average English gentleman' (32) and Wilson echoing many in depicting Waverley as 'colourless and feeble' (47). The stuff of Edward, therefore, is less action than reaction, less will than wimp.

Almost as old as this deprecation of his allegedly lacking human qualities, however, is the warm appreciation of Edward's role in the novel's plot and intellectual syntax. In 1815, Crabb Robinson was perhaps the first to note that Waverley, 'as his name was probably intended to indicate, is ever hesitating between two kings and two mistresses'; and in 1823, Alexis saw him not only as the thread running through the plot but as a proxy travelling for us – equally non-outstanding – readers, allowing us to test out 'how we would have felt or have acted in similar situations'. In this century, Buchan has seen him as a 'standpoint from which to view the whimsicalities and the heroics of the other characters' (133), Lukács as 'a perfect instrument for Scott's way of presenting the totality of certain transitional stages of history' (35), Johnson as a figure whose 'divided feelings are in essence exploratory of the issues' (525), Wilson as a 'carrier of our own exploration into his adventures' (47) and Shaw as allowing us 'to explore a wide range of social forms and historical beliefs' (188). Mere reactor and foil Edward may be, but he reacts and is foil to so much as to be the reader's essential intermediary.

Now, if this combination of trait and task is what constitutes a 'Waverley hero', then it must first be said that it embodies a paradox: one cannot praise Edward's role in the plot in the above terms while at the same time belittling his human qualities, because such a role cannot be fulfilled without some admirable human strengths. There is no intrinsic merit in vacillation or naïvety. But (as today's university students frequently point out) Edward is not devoid of characteristics much admired and required in our age of the dogma and the doctrinaire: he has the open-mindedness to go and see for himself, a facility for striking up contact once there, an ability to inquire *and* listen – *and* a willingness to change his mind when proved wrong.

The waverer is a type both common and dangerous and Scott shows its danger, both for Edward and for his troop. The non-waverer is a type equally dangerous, and – in the prejudiced Talbot and the fanatical Gilfillan – Scott intimates its aberrations also.

Were Edward to be a Talbot and not possess the ability to deal with people as varied as Bradwardine, from whom he 'differed *toto coelo*' (57), Fergus, Melville, Evan Dhu, Jinker and even Mrs Nosebag, neither would the plot's journeys be credible nor the encounters with the broad cast fruitful. A novel is, as Raymond Williams taught, a 'structure of feeling' and Scott, for all his Toryism, had a sovereign breadth of human sympathy, of which Edward is here the bearer and the reader, the beneficiary.

Secondly, however, if the above combination of trait and task is what makes a 'Waverley hero', then it must also be said that Waverley himself never was one. Mediator and man of middling virtue Edward may be: mediocre he is not. As close readers of the novel have pointed out, Edward is not only 'naturally modest' (31), a 'romantic and at the same time inquisitive youth' (30) with a 'spirited curiosity' (75), but is attested by Scott to have both 'powers of apprehension uncommonly quick, as almost to resemble intuition' (12) and 'at all times remarkable powers of conversation' (170), by the Edinburgh company to have 'powers of fancy, intelligence and eloquence' (209) and by the Chevalier to be 'though somewhat romantic, one of the most fascinating young men whom I have ever seen' (210). Even the arch-critical Flora, is struck latterly by his brilliance in society (209), by his 'talents and genius' (249).

If one asks why these abilities have often been ignored, the reason is one of the major weaknesses of the novel: a marked discrepancy between telling and showing. We are *told* of Edward's intelligence, told he is a brilliant talker, told he is fine dancer, but rarely is any of these talents *shown*. S. Stewart Gordon is right to insist that one must 'make a distinction between Waverley's appropriateness to the action and his vividness in that action' (Devlin, 1968, 82) and that it would not have harmed the novel had the latter been as strong as the former.

In what is still the best study of this issue, *The Hero of the*

Waverley Novels (1963), Alexander Welsh points out a further flaw in the traditional image of a passive and neutral 'Waverley hero' – namely, that he 'is not a neutral. He stands committed to prudence and the superiority of civil society. That commitment alone makes him a passive hero' (70). Indeed, it must be added that, on the second half of his travels, Edward is not passive either. From Ullswater onwards, each of his journeys is made on his own decision. And as early as Prestonpans he acts on his own initiative on the side of civil society, first rescuing Talbot and then attempting to save Colonel G—. The notion of a passive Edward meets neither the particulars of his case nor the nature of his active passiveness.

This is not to agree with those critics who claim that Edward thus becomes to some extent 'a hero in the true sense'. To be outstanding is not to be a hero. Indeed, Edward, outstanding in reading, talking and dancing, is outstanding in areas which precisely do *not* make one a hero, or at least not in the habitual meaning of the term. More fitting would seem the judgement of Alexis, who – as early as 1823 – termed Scott's protagonists 'anti-heroes'.

It is perhaps helpful here to place Edward within the cartography of the modern mind as mapped by Hegel. For Hegel's *Phenomenology of Mind* (1807) was not only published while Scott was at work on *Waverley* but covers the development of consciousness over the ages and stages Scott's novel portrays. Edward, for all his attraction to the clans, does not fully develop the 'heroism of dumb service' which Evan Dhu still displays. Nor, for all his wavering, is he the 'self-estranged mind' depicted in Diderot's *Le Neveu de Rameau* (1761) or Goethe's *The Sorrows of Young Werther* (1774). From Ullswater on, however, he does exhibit what Hegel describes as a transitional stage between the above two – that 'heroism of flattery' in which an individual becomes aware of the external power of society and of the prudential need to pay respects to it. It is in the renunciations and accommodations involved in that position that Edward achieves what (anti-)heroism he has.

Nor, given Edward's family background and family history, would one expect more. The Waverleys of old, for sure, did their bit in the Crusades, the Wars of the Roses and the Civil War, but even the crusading Wilibert of Waverley exhibited fateful dilatoriness, tarrying so long in the Holy Land that he returned to find his betrothed marrying another (a tale made much of in perhaps the first literary offspring of *Waverley*, Eliza Francis's romance *Sir Wilibert de Waverley; or, The Bridal Eve* (1815)). And by 1745, with Edward's own father, Richard, being an opportunist politician and with Sir Everard, the uncle to whom much of his upbringing is entrusted, having been more cagey than courageous in the Fifteen, the family's heroic days are long past.

In that same upbringing, however, other seeds are being sown. With a father leaning heavily to Hanover and an uncle heavily to Stuart, with tutors not leaning on him enough and with a family library leaning to amplitude and amusement; without a mother, who died when he was eleven, and with a father who is more intent on self than son, Edward grows up if not a waif then a waif in direction and discipline. He develops that 'wavering and unsettled habit of mind which is most averse to study and rivetted attention' (31); learns 'little of what adds dignity to man, and qualifies him to support and adorn an elevated situation in society' (14); has little 'skill to command and arrange' (15), imagination being 'the predominant faculty of his mind' (16) – grows, in other words into just that rudderless skiff that the novel's plot demands. As the *British Critic* nicely put it in August 1814:

> his wanderings are not gratuitous, nor is he wavering and indecisive only because the author chooses to make him so. Every feature of his character is formed by education, and it is to this first source that we are constantly referred for a just and sufficient cause of all the wandering passions as they arise in his mind.

It is common to see this education as a negative process, and certainly Edward himself deplores the fact that 'a thousand circumstances of fatal self-indulgence have made me the creature rather of imagination than of reason' (131). He becomes the archetypal shilly-shallier, the spin-it-out procrastinator, taking decisions on whim or letting events decide for him until, as

Fergus tells him before Prestonpans, 'All other reflections are now TOO LATE' (223).

It makes sense, however, to compare this education with that of Harley, hero of Henry Mackenzie's *The Man of Feeling* (1771), both because this too helps to 'place' Edward and because it brings out his more positive qualities. Harley too is somewhat parentless, his education 'but indifferently attended to' (XII), he too therefore 'a child in the drama of the world' (XIII). Indeed, Harley would be something of a progenitor of Edward, were not Edward, reaching adulthood in 1745, something of a forerunner of Harley. As Donald Davie and others have pointed out, Edward's nature, and especially his future as depicted by Flora –

> And he will refit the old library in the most exquisite Gothic taste, and garnish its shelves with the rarest and most valuable volumes; and he will draw plans and landscapes, and write verses, and rear temples, and dig grottoes; – and he will stand in a clear summer night in the colonnade before the hall, and gaze on the deer as they stray in the moonlight, or lie shadowed by the boughs of the old fantastic oaks; – and he will repeat verses to his beautiful wife, who shall hang upon his arm ... (250)

– are vignettes of the imminent Age of Sentiment. *Waverley* is dedicated on its final page to Henry Mackenzie and although there could be several reasons for this – Mackenzie's Addisonian prose, his sketches of manners, his support for *Waverley*'s early chapters – it may be that Scott was acknowledging Edward to be himself a 'man of feeling' (a figure more modern than some of his disparagers, but one who has had the satisfaction of outliving them).

Between Edward and Harley, however, there is a salient difference: whereas Harley succumbs to his sentience, dying partly as a result of his unworldliness, Edward survives and prospers. He is shown to have the merits of his failings – the curiosity to match his romancing, the empathy to match his fancifulness. Scott even remarks nicely that 'this compound of intense curiosity and exalted imagination forms a peculiar species of courage' (181). It seems unlikely that Scott considers this education (which has some parallels to his own) wholly harmful. Among the myriad travellers who traverse the pages of literature, Edward is not the quester or roamer, but the time-traveller between the ages and stages which make up his present, the sentient tourist to the foreign cultures within his own 'united' kingdom. Those who need convincing as to how literarily useful and humanly beneficial his merits are should cast a quick glance at previous fiction of the Rising.

10 Previous fiction of the Forty-five

a theme, perhaps the finest that could be selected, for fictitious composition *Redgauntlet*, xxiii

Waverley is not the earliest fiction of the Forty-five. Nor is its best-known predecessor, *The History of Tom Jones* (1749). To look briefly, however, at both Fielding and *his* predecessors is to shed some light on the quality of Scott's novel and of its protagonist.

Tom Jones too journeys through England in 1745, he too intends to fight for the Crown, and his story too repeatedly touches on the Rising. There, however, his own similarities with Edward and his *History*'s similarities with *Waverley* end. For the Rising is rarely in the forefront and Tom's stance on it is unwavering anyway: as a 'hearty well-wisher to the glorious cause of liberty, and of the Protestant religion', he volunteers for army service at Hambrook in Book 7, xi. And though his subsequent journeys take him no farther north than Coventry, let alone across the border, so that he never encounters the Chevalier and his forces, he does not scruple to speak of the Prince as 'the son of that very King James, a profest Papist, more bigotted, if possible, than his father' (8, xiv). Nor are the Jacobite sympathisers in the plot – say, the squire, whose horse is named 'Chevalier' – allowed really to contest him. In Fielding, who had pilloried the Rising in his two weeklies *The True Patriot* and *The Jacobite's Journal*, this is unsurprising, but it adds neither to our understanding of the rebellion nor to the stature of his work.

A far more central role is allotted to the Rising in *Alexis; or, The Worthy Unfortunate* (1747), an anonymous epistolary novel portraying the effects of the rebels' passage through Lancashire. In this story of pillage and fear, the ill-fated protagonist, Harry Sydenham, a battered and then neglected child, is robbed of his wife by La Serre, a French Colonel in the rebel ranks. Here too the rhetoric is firmly Hanoverian, the rebels being 'the Hellish Crew from the North' (12), the Chevalier 'this cursed Pretender' (8) and those English who join him 'silly Papists, rascally Non-jurors, and other idle and disorderly fellows' (9). The portrait of La Serre as villain (in contrast to Scott's figure of fun, M. de Beaujeu) is characteristic of a work in which images are confirmed rather than questioned.

The title of Sydenham's tale presumably owes something to an even earlier, and even more lurid anonymous novel of the Rising, *Alexis; or, The Young Adventurer* (1746), a rather arch and abruptly-ending *roman à clef*, in which Alexis is the Chevalier and Sa—gui—ius, the Duke of Cumberland. Here, rape and butchery of the wounded are commonplace but the luridness is at the expense of Hanover, its army being portrayed as a 'Pack of Bloodhounds' (5), while of the Rising it is claimed that 'Never was there a scheme of more Disinterestedness, an Enterprise of greater Danger' (3).

The above works are not to be confused with one of the best-known tracts of the time, *Ascanius; or, The Young Adventurer; a True History* (1746), which, purporting to be the first account of the fate of the Chevalier after Culloden, enjoyed a brief European vogue and notoriety. Mention of it, however, is not inappropriate, for although it claims on its title page to be 'Translated from a Manuscript privately handed about at the Court of Versailles' it is better described – as it was in the equally anonymous *Genuine and True Journal of the most miraculous escape of the Young Chevalier* (1749) – as 'composed of a very few facts, and the rest made up of Falsities and Fiction, the work of a fruitful brain', and promptly received an even earlier retort in *The Wanderer; or, Surprizing Escape* (1747). The classical allusion in its title is characteristic of a period in which historiography could be couched in 'Vulgar Rhyme', like Dougall Graham's oft-reprinted *Unpartial History of the Rise, Progress and Extinction of the Late Rebellion in*

England and Scotland (1747), or, like the anonymous *Chronicle of Charles the Young Man* (n.d.) and James Ray's famed *Acts of the Rebels* (1746), in mock-biblical prose. In fact, both the early 'histories' and the early fictions of the Forty-five are a wild maze of partisan claim and counter-claim, with the hedges between fact and fiction being often broken down.

With the exception of the second, all the above works are in Sir Walter's own library – of *Ascanius* he had at least five editions or versions – and it is possible that in publishing *Waverley* anonymously he was, not least, making a wry allusion to a publishing tradition against which his own work stands out all the more. Before *Waverley*, there is no plot which covers as much ground in 1745 as Edward, no protagonist as curious and unprejudiced, and thus no novel offering the manifold mediations Scott has in store.

11 Between highland and lowland, stasis and change

Yet if we look at modern events, we must not too hastily venture to conclude that our own times have so much the superiority over former days as we might at first be tempted to infer.

Preface to *Auchindrane*

Edward is an intermediary firstly between lowland and highland, change and stasis, tomorrow and yesteryear. The estates between which he escorts the reader – Waverley Honour, Tully-Veolan and Glennaquoich – can be seen also as states or stages of civilization. Yet, having rejected the old ways of Glennaquoich he opts not for the more modern ways of his English home but for a restored Tully-Veolan beside a pacified highland line, with a Scotswoman as wife and the daughter of a highland robber as her *fille de chambre*. The triadic pattern, the synthesis, the choice of the interim on the outer edge are all clear. The mediation is also an adjudication, but as such it demands an act of understanding.

That Edward turns away from Glennaquoich might seem easily understood: after all, it languishes in what Ferguson in his *Essay on the History of Civil Society* calls the 'barbarous state'. Indeed, Section II, 3 of the *Essay* – 'Of Rude Nations under the Impressions of Property and Interest' – is an inventory of the Mac-Ivor clan:

> They are still averse to labour, addicted to war, admirers of fortitude, and, in the language of Tacitus, more lavish of their blood than of their sweat. They are fond of fantastic ornaments in their dress, and endeavour to fill up the listless intervals of a life addicted to violence, with hazardous sports and with games of chance. Every servile occupation they commit to women or slaves ... The members of any community, being distinguished among themselves by unequal shares in the distribution of property, the ground of a permanent and palpable subordination is laid.

The scant agriculture, the virtual absence of enclosure, the institutional idleness, the rugged athletics and games, the military training, the cult of valour, the leaving of menial tasks to women, the plaid, trews, kilt and clan tartan (on the last two of which Scott may be anachronistic), the overall note of primitive 'rudeness' – in all these ways Scott's Glennaquoich is Ferguson localized, detailed, made flesh.

Moreover, this is true especially of 'palpable subordination' – of what Hegel's *Phenomenology* terms the 'heroism of dumb service' – for Scott correctly portrays the clans of 1745 as feudal, 'each headed by their patriarchal ruler' (119). And over Clan Mac-Ivor rules its chieftain, Fergus, than whom, Scott remarks, 'few men were more attached to ideas of chieftainship and feudal power' (89). From the 'tail' or entourage which sometimes accompanies him – his devoted retainer Evan Dhu lovingly counts on his fingers its several members (75) – to the seating at the clan feast, Glennaquoich is rigidly patriarchal. Not only can Fergus boast during the Rising that he 'brought in all the Perthshire men when not one would have stirred' (252), but when his clan charges at Prestonpans it is to the cry 'Forward, sons of Ivor' (223).

For Scott the lawyer, this structure has an unlovely side. 1745 is no longer 1715 and *Waverley* is not *Rob Roy*, where, in Baillie Jarvie's words 'the never another law hae they but the length o' their dirks' (*RR* 26). But given Fergus's 'hasty, haughty, and vindictive temper' (90) and given the fact that even the Chevalier is loath 'to encroach on the patriarchal authority of the chieftains, of which they were very jealous' (271), clan law is subject to something Scott always assails – arbitrariness. The young Callum Beg, struck down for 'acting without orders and lying to disguise it' (269) on the march south, is the victim the novel portrays. On Edward's asking how he could mete out such punishment to one so young, Fergus replies, 'Why, if I did not strike hard sometimes, the rascals would forget themselves' (278).

For Scott the economic and social historian, however, the clans have further weaknesses. Significantly, when highlanders first enter the novel it is in the *creagh*, the rustling of Tully-Veolan cattle designed to ensure the payment of blackmail. And equally significantly, the first hospitality Edward receives beyond the highland line is in the cave of Donald Bean Lean, a robber, and his first breakfast is made from meal and eggs begged or borrowed from distant cottagers. These first experiences are the highland economy *in nuce*. Fergus's power rests on a deliberate policy of over-population both sustained by and sustaining war:

> His own patriarchal power he strengthened at every expence which his fortune would permit, and indeed stretched his means to the uttermost to maintain the rude and plentiful hospitality, which was the most valued attribute of a chieftain. For the same reason, he crowded his estate with a tenantry, hardy indeed, and fit for the purposes of war, but greatly outnumbering what the soil was calculated to maintain. (92)

Throughout, the highlanders of 1745 are either predators or parasites on a culture more successful than their own.

For all these demerits, however, one should not forget what Ferguson also wrote of the 'barbarous state': 'Even under this description mankind are generous and hospitable to strangers ... friendship and enmity are to them terms of the greatest importance' (II, 3). This too Scott memorably shows: in the warmth with which Edward is received, in the solidarity of the clansmen, in the total self-abandon with which Evan Dhu is prepared, at Carlisle, to die in his chief's stead. The clan toasts which resound at the Glennaquoich feast –

'To him that will not turn his back on friend or foe.' 'To him that never forsook a comrade.' 'To him that never bought or sold justice.' 'Hospitality to the exile and broken bones to the tyrant.' 'The lads in the kilts.' 'Highlanders shoulder to shoulder.' (98)

– are shown by events to have their grounding in reality. When at the novel's end Scott looks back elegiacally on the world that has been lost, on 'many living examples of singular and disinterested attachment to the principles of loyalty which they received from their fathers, and of old Scottish faith, hospitality, worth and honour' (340), he is referring not least to the firmly-bonded *Gemeinschaft* of the clans, in which 'a kinsman is part of a man's body, but a foster-brother is a piece of his heart' (112).

Nor can it be overlooked that within this 'barbarous state' there is the extant oral culture of the *bhaird*, which exerts a great fascination on Edward, and that among these kinsmen there are two to whom Edward is strongly and understandably drawn. Fergus may be calculating and short-fused, but he is also a man of education, depth and *esprit*, courage, drive and *savoir-faire*. (One of the features of teaching *Waverley* at university is that students often line up on his side.) Flora is quite the most imposing character in the work, a *pasionaria* in her beliefs, a quick-silver in her judgements, a virtuoso in her arts, a well-spring in her nature.

When, therefore, Edward turns away from the clans, it is probably for the mundanest of reasons: they too have no resistance to the onward march of time. It is with them that the novel's sense of lastness is most pervading. The clan seer, Donnacha an Amrigh, is dead (81); the clan bard who sings at the feast is aged; Flora learns the harp from Rory Dall, 'one of the last harpers of the Western Highlands' (106); and Fergus, who regards the feast as a 'barbarous ritual of our forefathers' (102) sees himself too as an increasing anachronism: ' "there are three things that are useless to a modern Highlander, – a sword which he must not draw, – a bard to sing of deeds which he dare not imitate, – and a large goat-skin purse without a louis-d'or to put into it" ' (103). Worse still, he maintains his army only under permit – to assist the government in preserving peace in the Highlands. The long arm of lowland London is already reaching into his glen. The maxim of the new age, he himself acknowledges, is 'Better an old woman with a purse in her hand than three men with belted brands' (97).

As always in Scott, time is the strongest agent the novel contains and Edward turns away from Glennaquoich not because it is wrong, but because it is no longer possible, since untimely.

But why does he not return to a way of life which clearly *is* possible, that of southern England? After all, on returning to England after the Rising, Edward feels 'that pleasure which almost all feel who return to a verdant, populous, and highly-cultivated country, from scenes of waste desolation, or of solitary grandeur' (329). To Scott, such vistas are an essential indicator: he is not one of those to cry 'Enclosure, thou art a blight upon the land' – on the contrary, he comments favourably on enclosure in *Guy Mannering* and *Redgauntlet* and notes its virtual absence at both Glennaquoich and Tully-Veolan, where 'the unprofitable variety of the surface resembled a tailor's book of patterns' (34). Equally, when Edward left Waverley-Honour, it was impressed on him that he could not be accompanied by a body of retainers (25) – could not, in other words, deploy in England the destructive potential of a Fergus. Both for Edward, the young aristocrat and man of feeling, and for Scott, the improver and lover of civil peace, Waverley-Honour might thus have seemed the obvious choice of home.

Such a choice, however, would tend to ignore an undertone in the novel which looks askance at some aspects of the new age coming from the South. It is an age of dishonourable self-interest, as exemplified in Edward's father, Richard, turn-coat MP for the tell-tale constituency of Barterfaith. It is an age of money, of what Bradwardine half-jokingly calls the '*Diva Pecunia* of the Southron' (333). And it is an age of law, as embodied in the unlovable Mr Clippurse, whose firm merges during the novel to form Messrs Clippurse and Hookem. Moreover, in the shape of the niggardly pettifogger Baillie Macwheeble – who, as Scott intimates, could be from the clan of Wheedle or Quibble (44) – the latter trend at least is encroaching on Scotland.

All considered, therefore, the location and restored state of Tully-Veolan make it a symbolically apt abode for Edward to take up. It stands for two of the central values of the work – a wary acknowledgement of change and a need for an awareness of origins.

12 Between prejudice and cultural tolerance

> Less liked he still that scornful jeer
> Misprized the land he loved so dear
>
> *The Lay of the Last Minstrel*, V, xxx

The *creagh* may be the first time highlanders enter the novel, but it is not the first time they are mentioned. Among the well-meaning advice his Aunt Rachael bestows upon Edward as he first leaves for Scotland are the following choice reflections:

> She allowed that the northern part of the island contained some ancient families, but they were all whigs and presbyterians except the Highlanders; and respecting them she must needs say, there could be no great delicacy among the ladies, where the gentlemen's attire was, as she had been assured, to say the least, very singular, and not at all decorous. (30)

Such expressions of prejudice are characteristic of *Waverley*, in which the very word 'prejudice' occurs frequently: Mr Pembroke declares Scotland to be 'utter darkness' (28), the dying Houghton still views highlanders as 'wild petticoat men' (218) and Evan Dhu, in turn, is convinced of 'the effeminacy of the Lowlanders, and particularly of the English' (77). Equally characteristic, however, is that Edward's curiosity helps him to rise above such attitudes, his journeys and mediation being in service also of cultural learning and tolerance.

The issue of prejudice is so important to Scott that he makes it a major trait of a key figure in his plot: Colonel Talbot. Talbot has been called 'the most nearly perfect' of the novel's cast (Davie, 31), and certainly he is the model of probity and altruism. Scott, however, squarely depicts him as 'the English gentleman and soldier, manly, open, and generous, but not unsusceptible of prejudice against those of a different country, or who opposed him in political tenets' (240). So anti-Scottish is Talbot in fact that 'he looks as if he thought no Scottish-woman worth the trouble of handing her a cup of tea' (249). He himself jokes that 'he could not have endured Venus herself, if she had been announced in a drawing-room by the name of Miss Mac-Jupiter' (247). The gist of the plot, however, is that such prejudice has a less than jocular side.

Consider the following exchange between Talbot and Edward just after Edward has secured a free pass from the Chevalier allowing Talbot to leave captivity and travel to London to his ailing wife:

> 'But I see your Highland friend Glen— what do you call his barbarous name? and his orderly with him. I must not call him his orderly cut-throat any more, I suppose. See how he walks as if the world were his own, with the bonnet on one side of his head, and his plaid puffed out across his breast. I should like now to meet that youth where my hands were not tied: I would tame his pride or he should tame mine.'
>
> 'For shame, Colonel Talbot; you swell at sight of the tartan, as the bull is said to do at scarlet. You and Mac-Ivor have some points not much unlike, so far as national prejudice is concerned.'
>
> The latter part of this discourse passed in the street. They passed the Chief, the Colonel punctiliously and he sternly greeting each other, like two duellists before they take their ground. It was evident the dislike was mutual. 'I never see that surly dog at his heels,' said the Colonel, after he had mounted his horse, 'but he reminds me of lines I have somewhere heard – upon the stage, I think:
>
> — 'Close behind him
> Stalks sullen Bertram, like a sorcerer's fiend,
> Pressing to be employed.'
>
> 'I assure you that you judge too harshly of the Highlanders.'
>
> 'Not a whit, not a whit; I cannot spare them a jot; I cannot bate them an ace. Let them stay in their own barren mountains, and puff and swell, and hang their bonnets on the horns of the moon if they have a mind; but what business have they to come where people wear breeches and speak an intelligible language – I mean intelligible in comparison to their gibberish, for even the Lowlanders talk a kind of English little better than the Negroes in Jamaica. I pity the Pre— I mean the Chevalier himself, for having so many desperadoes about him. And they learn their trade so early. There is a kind of subaltern imp, for example, a sort of sucking devil, whom your friend Glena— Glenamuck

there, has sometimes in his train. To look at him he is about fifteen years; but he is a century old in mischief and villainy. He was playing at quoits the other day in the court; a gentleman, a decent-looking person enough, came past, and as a quoit hit his shin, he lifted his cane: But my young bravo whips out his pistol, like Beau Clincher in the Trip to the Jubilee, and had not a shrill scream of *Gardez l'eau*, from an upper window, set all parties a-scampering for fear of the inevitable consequences, the poor gentleman would have lost his life by the hands of that little cockatrice.'

'A fine character you'll give of Scotland upon your return, Colonel Talbot.'

'O, Justice Shallow shall save me the trouble – Barren, barren, beggars all, beggars all. Marry, good air, – and that only when you are out of Edinburgh, and not yet come to Leith, as is our case at present.'

In a short time they arrived at the seaport. (262–63)

The passage is an early example of the several strengths which are to become Scott the historical novelist's stock-in-trade: the effortless inclusion of social detail (the outdoor sports, the slop-emptying, the noisome Edinburgh air); the self-portrayal and self-exposure of character through conversation; and the sovereign good humour, even comedy, through which a high seriousness can emerge – in this case the utter seriousness of an analysis of cultural arrogance.

As Talbot warms to his self-appointed task, he does not shrink from moving from mere abuse (barbarous, cut-throat), through demonization (fiend, devil) to scatalogical innuendo (Glenamuck) and racism (Negroes). The tirade is masterly in its rabid arrogation of cultural superiority while every utterance suggests a different interpretation. The postulation of breeches as the only valid male attire and southern English as the only intelligible tongue are ethnocentrism on the rampage. One can understand the demure Scottish Rose terming such a man 'a very disagreeable person, to be sure' (249).

The deadening enormity of Talbot's position becomes apparent, however, only when seen in its various contexts. This is a man who has just received a free pass from the Chevalier, a man who will yet condone the executions at Carlisle, a man who in this respect is the less than acceptable face of the victors. Elsewhere, Scott remarks that Talbot reveals 'those prejudices which are peculiarly English' (246) and here delivers them a two-fold rebuff: in a nice irony, he allows Talbot unwittingly to liken himself to Justice Shallow and then allows Edward a rare opportunity to deploy the rhetorical skills we are told he has. Given that the phrase entered the English language only around 1810, this may well be the first attribution of 'national prejudice' in high literature.

It is fitting to juxtapose the above exchange with that between Edward and Fergus at Carlisle, just prior to the executions:

> 'We part not *here*?' said Waverley.
>
> 'O yes, we do, you must come no farther. Not that I fear what is to follow for myself,' he said proudly, 'Nature has her tortures as well as art, and how happy should we think the man who escapes from the throes of a mortal and painful disorder, in the space of a short half hour? And this matter, spin it out as they will, cannot last longer. But what a dying man can suffer firmly, may kill a living friend to look upon. – This same law of high treason,' he continued with astonishing firmness and composure, 'is one of the blessings, Edward, with which your free country has accommodated poor old Scotland – her own jurisprudence, as I have heard, was much milder. But I suppose one day or other – when there are no longer any wild Highlanders to benefit from its tender mercies – they will blot it from their records, as levelling them with a nation of cannibals. The mummery, too, of exposing the senseless head – they have not the wit to grace mine with a paper coronet; there would be some satire in that, Edward. I hope they will set it on the Scotch gate though, that I may look, even after death, to the blue hills of my own country, that I love so dearly. The Baron would have added,
>
> 'Moritur, et moriens dulces reminiscitur Argos.'
>
> A bustle, and the sound of wheels and horses' feet, was now heard in the court-yard of the castle. (326–27)

There is a searing sadness in these lines and it is a sadness born of ironies. There is the little irony of Fergus, not always the most just of men, here implying injustice. And there are the greater ironies of the grace, the aphoristic poise, the classical education of the alleged barbarian; of the barbaric means of his execution imposed by the ostensibly civilizing nation; of the Scots' own tradition (ended just after the Union) being the milder; of the Talbots triumphing over the Mac-Ivors.

These and other passages are a plea for cultural understanding and cultural tolerance. In this respect, Scott's historical novel is the literary heir of Herder's *Geschichtsphilosophie* with its revolutionary sense for the integrity of foreign cultures and its call for intercultural empathy – and the legacy is expressed in the novel's very form. Just as the papal legate, in Scott's anecdote, corrects his opinion that 'Scotland was the – the latter end of the world' on actually experiencing a highland feast (115), so Waverley's journeys are the doubly appropriate form of cultural travel for an age of Empire abroad and little mobility at home. It was partly to this that Hazlitt was referring in *The Spirit of the Age* (1825) when claiming that the 'candour of Sir Walter's historic pen levels our bristling principles' freeing the mind from the petty, the narrow, and the bigoted (Hayden, 286–7).

13 Between rebellion and civil order, nationhood and Union

I hope we shall have no war of so unnatural and unchristian a kind in our time *The Black Dwarf*, II

Most famously, of course, Edward takes the reader not only from the pacific South to the uneasy North, but also into the very teeth of the Forty-five Rising. As such, his journey – and it is significantly this which many of his European successors seek to emulate – becomes vicarious experience of, and a disquisition on, rebellion and civil order.

Repeatedly Waverley is shown the social cost of rebellion. There are, for sure, those to whom others' cost is personal profit: the irrepressible Edinburgh landlady Mrs Flockhart 'cared not how long the rebellion lasted that brought her into company so much above her usual associates' (202). But for most, as Bradwardine grimly remarks, the sinews of war are less easily found than its flesh and blood. Edward witnesses the carcases and carrion crows at Clifton, the 'broken carriages, dead horses, unroofed cottages, trees felled for palisades, and bridges destroyed or only partially repaired' (295) that strew his subsequent journey north, and then the despoliation of Tully-Veolan. Even Mrs Flockhart opens her door to find one of her new associates in a different state:

> 'The poor Hieland body, Dugald Mahoney, cam here a while since wi' ane of his arms cut off, and a sair clour in the head – ye'll mind Dugald, he carried aye an axe on his shoulder – and he cam here just begging, as I may say, for something to eat.' (294)

On the virtues of such scenes neither Edward nor the novel is ever in doubt: even before Prestonpans, Edward feels 'inexpressible repugnance at being accessary to the plague of civil war' (140). In 1814, however, it was probably less the views of neophyte Edward than those of Talbot, fresh from campaigns on the European mainland, which would have echoed in the mind. His very first words to Edward are:

> 'I am not so inexperienced a soldier, sir, ... as to complain of the fortune of war. I am only grieved to see those scenes acted in our own island, which I have often witnessed elsewhere with comparative indifference.' (233)

With both the Napoleonic campaigns and the French Revolution still uppermost in the memory, Scott the patriot and Scott the social Tory are here sounding an unmistakably minatory note. Certainly that was how the reviewer in the *British Critic* read the work, hoping that the 'history of those bloody days' would 'by an early and awful warning inspire the nation with a jealous vigilance against the very first symptoms of their recurrence'.

Nor is there any doubt as to the novel's verdict on the actual feasibility of the Forty-five: after Derby, Fergus himself counsels Edward to disassociate himself, arguing that 'the vessel is going to pieces, and it is full time for all who can to get into the long-boat to leave her' (275), and Flora at Carlisle, grievously regretting her part in egging her brother on, nevertheless expresses it with characteristic lucidity: 'I do not regret his attempt because it was wrong: O no, on that point I am armed; but because it was impossible it could end otherwise than thus' (323).

But there's the rub: feasibility is not desirability. And a work of literature is more than the sum of its plot's outcomes.

Beneath the issue of rebellion or civil order is another which prompts and dogs much of Scott's Scottish fiction – long and short – and much else in his *oeuvre* besides: the issue of nationhood or Union. And here his adjudication is far more equivocal, his loyalties far more strained and wavering.

In general, the nearer in setting Scott's Scottish novels are to the Union of 1707, the more contested that Union is: thus in *The Heart of Midlothian*, set in 1737, a Scots seamstress exclaims, 'Weary on Lunnon, and a' that e'er came out o't! ... they hae taken awa our parliament, and they hae oppressed our trade' (*HM* 4); in *Rob Roy*, set in 1715–16, Andrew Fairservice speaks repeatedly of the 'sad and sorrowfu' Union' (*RR* 18); and in *The Black Dwarf*, set in the Union's immediate aftermath, Mareschal longs for 'some amends on the Unionist courtiers that have bought and sold old Scotland' (*BD* 12) and there is a veritable litany on the theme of Scotland's having been 'at once cheated of her independence, her commerce, and her honour' (*BD* 13). But however vexed his characters may be, Scott their author balances 'their' anti-Union statements with 'his' pro-Union commentary – arguing 'how little it seemed for some time to promise the beneficial results which have since taken place' (*BD* 2), stating that 'the Union had, indeed, opened to Scotland the trade of the English colonies' (*RR* 19) and regretting that 'the national league, so important to the safety of both, was in the utmost danger of being dissolved' (*HM* 35). It would be a bold interpreter who could say which, character or commentator, is a more important corrective to whom.

A similarly ambivalent stance is found in Scott's other writings. It has been claimed by P. H. Scott (73) that the most Scott ever wrote in favour of the Union is tucked away in a letter to Maria Edgeworth of July 1825. But that is not so: at the conclusion of his brief *Description of the Regalia of Scotland* (1819), Scott writes:

> We who now reap the slow, but well ripened fruits of the painful sacrifice made at the Union, can compare, with calmer judgement, the certain blessings of equality of laws and rights, extended commerce, improved agriculture, individual safety, and domestic peace, with the

> vain, though generous boast of a precarious national independence, subject to all the evils of domestic faction and delegated oppression. With such feelings we look upon the Regalia of Scotland, venerating at once the gallantry of our forefathers, who with unequal means, but with unsubdued courage, maintained the liberties and independence of Scotland through ten centuries of almost ceaseless war; and blessing the wise decrees of Providence, which, after a thousand years of bloodshed, have at length indissolubly united the two nations, who, speaking the same language, professing the same religion, and united in the same interests, seemed formed by GOD and Nature to compose one people. (*RS* 33–4)

On the other hand, just seven years later, in the blistering, Swiftian assault of his *Letters of Malachi Malagrowther*, Scott does not shrink from dubbing England the 'foreign *enemy*' (*MM* II,14), a power which treats the Scots as 'the Spaniards treated the Indians' with the result that 'we have become the caterpillars of the island, instead of its pillars' (*MM* II, 66). Taking their stand on the Scots' right to issue their own banknotes, the *Letters* are an impassioned call for cultural diversity:

> For God's sake, sir, let us remain as Nature made us, Englishmen, Irishmen, and Scotchmen, with something like the impress of our several countries upon each! ... The degree of national diversity between different countries, is but an instance of that general variety which Nature seems to have adopted as a principle through all her works, as anxious, apparently, to avoid, as modern statesmen to enforce, anything like an approach to absolute 'uniformity'. (*MM* II, 83–4)

If one considers *all* the above evidence, then one cannot baldly say with Lord Dacre that Scott 'believed passionately in the Union with England. He was a British patriot' (1971, 226). The ambivalence of Scott's stance demands at least a more balanced account – *perhaps* the formulation of Christopher Harvie, 'Scott's Jacobitism was sentimental; his attachment to the Union deep and sincere' (1983, 40), *perhaps* that of P. H. Scott, 'Once or twice Scott did express acceptance of the Union, but his acceptance was always reluctant, grudging and conditional' (73). It is a mark of how vexed the issue is, however, that even these two recent Scottish commentators place the emphasis in opposite scales.

In *Waverley* too, Union or not is the bottom line, and

although the work antedates all the above, both Scott and Edward reveal very much this same ambivalence: their dual desire for civil peace in the land and Scottishness north of the border leaves them political Unionists but cultural Jacobites. Those who see the Scott of *Waverley* as an apologist for the Union or a 'sort of jovial ideologue of progress' (Kerr, 21) must account for Talbot and Barterfaith. Those who see it as a plea for independence must account for the marital union at Tully-Veolan.

Such an ambivalent stance is a trait not only of *Waverley* but of the Romantic historical novel at large. Writing of Scott's immediate successors such as Hugo, de Vigny, Hauff and Tieck, and noting the prevalence in their work too of this same theme of rebellion, Paul-Michael Lützeler argues cogently that the theme arises from a 'twofold middle-class opposition' – opposition to the notion of any revolution *à la* 1789, but opposition also to the suppression of the demands of social liberation movements (234). Applied *mutatis mutandis* to the case of *Waverley*, this becomes a dislike both of the civil disorder brought about by rebellion and of the suppression of cultures, which can then issue in such disorder. For as Scott remarked in a renowned letter on the *Malachi* issue, 'If you unscotch us, you will find us damned mischievous Englishmen' (*L* IX, 471).

There is no need to try to 'resolve' the ambivalence in Scott's position. Those who would claim him unequivocally for one camp or the other might reflect that one of the reasons one becomes a novelist is presumably that one doesn't have a short answer to each and every question.

14 Between romance and realism

'View things as they are, and not as they might be magnified through thy teeming fantasy' *Redgauntlet*, Letter II

In literary and human terms, however, there is another way of expressing Scott's position on all the above issues: this is in terms of a polarity which informs many of his novels (notably *Guy Mannering*, *Redgauntlet* and *The Black Dwarf*) but is nowhere as marked as in *Waverley*, where it constitutes both a central metaphorical thread and the co-ordinates of Edward's final mediation – between romance and realism.

Edward is a readers' hero because he is a reader-hero. By nature, his author frequently records, he is 'wild and romantic in his ideas' (56), prompted on by the 'wild romance of his spirit' (65), but this has been fostered by the Waverley-Honour library, one of whose strengths is precisely romance – English, Italian and Spanish – and together bent and books have combined to produce the major weakness in his make-up. Though not as extreme as that former romance figure, Don Quixote, a tilter at windmills, Edward has developed what Scott terms 'that more common aberration from sound judgement, which apprehends occurrences indeed in their reality, but communicates to them a tincture of its own romantic tone and colouring' (18). Scott, who wrote in his *Memoirs* of 1808 that 'I really believe I have read as much nonsense of this class as any man now living' (Hewitt, 1981, 32), was no doubt in this portrait exercising self-criticism and many a reader honest enough to note that his or her own 'principle of reality' is not fully honed will find something of interest here.

Again and again in the first two volumes Edward applies his tincture to people and events. Having managed to find in the very unlovely Tully-Veolan village four girls who 'somewhat resembled Italian forms of landscape' (33), he feels after the *creagh* that he is 'actually in the land of military and romantic adventures' (72) and in Glennaquoich naturally sees himself as 'a knight of romance' courting the hand of Flora, 'a fair enchantress of Boiardo or Ariosto' (105–6). The human problem in this is that Edward tends to self-deception, becoming a hope-against-hoper, still hoping even in Edinburgh – after she has twice firmly rejected him - that he can gain Flora's favour. The political problem is that he allows himself to be similarly inveigled by the allure of Jacobitism, whose leader 'threw himself upon the mercy of his countreymen, rather like the hero of romance than a calculating politician' (206).

As Flora cuttingly remarks, however, 'Affection can (now and then) withstand very severe storms of rigour, but not a long polar frost of downright indifference' (257). And so it proves with Jacobitism too. On the long wintertime march south, its lustre gradually falls away until, after Clifton, Edward is prepared to leave the cause for the second time. After long lone walks by wintry Ullswater – the novel has something of the familiar seasonal patterning – he is able to fight free of his romancing tendency and feel 'entitled to say firmly, though perhaps with a sigh, that the romance of his life was ended, and that its real history had now commenced' (283).

His transition from romance to realism is dramatized in his transfer of affection from Flora to Rose. Flora is the bewitching romance figure, Rose, 'not precisely the sort of beauty or merit which captivates a romantic imagination in early youth' (66). This is not to say, however, that Rose is simply a come-down. Even more than Edward, she has suffered from a bad press (and for the same reason: her deeds are not shown). It must not be ignored that whereas Flora sends her brother to his death, Rose rescues Edward's life. Rose has the resourcefulness of the real, Flora the enthusiasms of fancy.

Again Scott uses eloquent naming and symbolic patterning to underscore his meaning here: Edward's romantic moonings in youth are located beside the gloriously named Mirkwood Mere. And what becomes of his copy of Ariosto, lent to Rose for edification? He finds it hurled to the ground from her lofty balcony, 'wasted by the wind and rain' (297), after Tully-Veolan has been plundered by English troops.

It seems unlikely that Scott intended to run down the romance state of mind completely: after all, one of the most likeable figures in the novel, the understanding and tolerant Revd Morton, has also been a reader with 'a slight feeling of romance, which no after incidents of real life had entirely dissipated' (162). Nevertheless, the thrust of the work is rather different from that of *The Man of Feeling*, whose protagonist Harley remarks, '"Perhaps we now-a-days discourage the romantic turn a little too much. Our boys are prudent too soon"' (XXXIII). It is one of the ironies of literary history that Scott, whose work is a repeated critique of romance, should be the among the authors read by Madame Bovary when Flaubert comes to criticize *her* reading habits. Such is the march of realism.

Waverley has been described as the first novel whose hero is a reader. The judgement is a bit hard on Werther and Rameau's nephew – to name but two – but Edward, who takes with him to Scotland 'the best English poets of every description and other works on belles lettres' (65) is certainly a reader sophisticated enough to see his life in literary-critical terms and thus to enrich the novel with a further level of meaning. The feudal Highlands, political Jacobitism, the Rising – these are the realm of romance. By 1745, however, even more than in 1707, it must be concluded, as often in Scott's early novels, that 'these are not the days of romance but of sad reality' (*BD* 6).

Chapter 3

Waverley as history

15 Historical fiction and history as temporal structures

were we to point out the most marked distinction between a real and a fictitious narrative ... Introduction to *The Abbot*

'Historical fiction is not history, but it springs from history and reacts upon it' (88): Trevelyan's words of 1921 are still an appropriate beginning. They remind one that historical fiction, notably in the case of Scott, has had a marked influence on historiography – so much so that one cannot do full justice to *Waverley* without placing it in its relationship both to history in general and to the developing history of the Forty-five. But this first entails investigating what historiography and historical fiction, for all their differences, have in common.

There is the past (*res gestae*) and there is history (*historia rerum gestarum*). As the Greek philosopher Agathon said, not even God can change the past – although many might like to. History, however, is not the past but an account of the past and is forever being re-written, the type or types of historical account written being also subject to development and change. History, as the great Dutch historian Pieter Geyl claimed, is 'a debate without end', so that what one reads is never 'the history of ...', but always '*a* history of ...'.

The essential similarity between histories and historical fictions is that both are (usually) narratives. Historians and philosophers of history alike agree that 'history tells stories' (Danto, 111), and that both history and novel attempt to achieve a narrative line which is 'followable'. Thus Michael Oakeshott has written: 'the historian, in short, is like the novelist, whose characters (for example) are presented in such detail that additional explanation of their actions is superfluous' (141).

This is not, of course, to say that history is the same *type* of followable story as a novel. The attempt of some post-modern theoreticians under the impact of Hayden White's *Metahistory* (1973) to assert that history is *solely* a story ignores that the narratives of historians, unlike those of novelists, have to satisfy the demands of verifiability. It is important to recognize the major creative effort of historians, but one should not throw out the historical baby with the story-telling bathwater. As Macaulay put it in his essay 'History' (1828), 'History begins in novel and ends in essay.' Or, in the more recent words of the American philosopher of history, Haskell Fain, 'A history without the right story is blind. The right story without a history is empty' (308). What it does mean, however, is that philosophy of history can provide terms in which the relationship between history and historical fiction can be clarified. A helpful term is A. C. Danto's 'temporal structure', by which is meant a structure imposed on *res gestae*, grouping some together with others, and ruling out some as lacking relevance. Such structures, Danto writes,

> are, of course, *ad hoc* in some degree. The identical event may indeed be a constituent in any number of different temporal structures: E may be collected with any number of otherwise disjointed collections of events into distinct temporal wholes. Thus our description of E may accordingly vary as we group it with different collections of events into different temporal structures. (6)

Danto's formulation is useful, firstly, because it does justice to the historian's creativity: the historian, in a great act of 'colligation', brings together a vast congeries of material to constitute a coherent version of E. Now, let E be the French Revolution (Danto's example) or the Forty-five. We can speak of innumerable Frenchmen or Scotsmen as engaged in 'French-Revolutionizing' or 'Forty-fiving' around 1789 or 1745. 'Forty-fiving' does not involve all people in Scotland at that time, and it involves some people not in Scotland. Nor were even those whom it does involve all of them all the time Forty-fiving. The Forty-five is thus exhibited discontinuously over Scottish and other soil and mid eighteenth-century time. Just what constitutes a satisfactory version of this E will depend on one's criteria of relevance, which will in turn influence and be influenced by the type of 'temporal structure' one has chosen.

A major factor here will be duration, which is interdependent with an essential issue in history: causation. As R. G. Collingwood wrote in *The Idea of Nature* (1945), historians give very different views of the past if they see an event as something that takes an hour, ten years or anything up to 1,000 years. He continues:

> We can even say to some extent what kind of differences there would be. In general, making things takes far longer than destroying them. The shorter our standard time-phase for an historical event, the more our history will consist of destructions, catastrophes, battle, murder and sudden death. But destruction implies the existence of something to destroy; and as this type of history cannot describe how such a thing came into existence, for the process of its coming into existence was a process too long to be conceived as an event by this type of history, its existence must be presupposed as given, ready-made, miraculously established by some force outside history. (25–6)

Thus a history of the Forty-five which began at Glenfinnan would offer a different aspect on the causes of the Rising from one beginning in 1743, which would differ again from one opening in 1715, 1707 or 1689. Duration, however, is not only a question of prior time: it is always our ignorance of the future which limits our understanding of the past and present, and a history of the Forty-five written sixty years since may differ greatly from one written one year since or written today. As Carlyle wrote in 'On History' (1838), 'Only in the combination of coming Time and Time come is the meaning of either completed.'

The usefulness here of these terms and considerations is that they are applicable also – perhaps *more* so – to literary forms. For what makes *Waverley* such a striking account of its E, the Forty-five, is precisely that it groups it with the otherwise disjointed to provide a different description of it – different from prior histories *and* different also from the visions of *res gestae* given in other forms of literary portrayal of the past. For the ballad or lay has a different temporal structure from that of the historical novel, which differs again from that of the historical tale or drama. In brief, the historical novel will *tend* – and these are only tendencies – to a more long-term, more richly casted, more 'democratic' vision of the past, the ballad will *tend* to a brief-span, more 'aristocratic' or feudal vision, and the historical drama or novella/*Novelle* will *tend* to see the past as determined by fewer historical agents. The historical novel is to the ballad as the campaign is to the battle; to the drama, as the army is to its leaders; and to the *Novelle*, as the multi-faceted social explanation is to the bald catastrophe.

The German critic Walter Benjamin argued in his essay 'The Story-teller' (1936) that 'Every study of a particular epic form must be concerned with the relationship of that form to history.' In history, as elsewhere, significance is relatedness, and the significance of *Waverley* – in both literary history and a history of history – is the more, or the other, it relates and the different manner of that relation.

16 The Forty-five: a modern history

'the late desperate and unhappy matter of 1745'

Redgauntlet, Letter IX

There are, therefore, as many Forty-fives as there are types of narrative and types of narrator to tell them, but a brief modern history of the Forty-five, based on later research but citing also contemporary accounts, might run something like this.

The Forty-five was not the first Jacobite rising, nor was it the gravest, but it was the last. Preceded by the severe Fifteen and the lesser Nineteen, and by earlier rumblings in 1708 and 1688–90, it was the last attempt of the Stuart dynasty and cause to establish its king on the English throne – after a lapse of some sixty years in exile and four Hanoverian reigns.

In the early 1740s circumstances in the three countries involved – Scotland, England and France – partly favoured a Jacobite attempt: for France the War of Austrian Succession (1740–6) made a disturbance on England's flank desirable; in England, there was great dissatisfaction among the Country faction, from whom the Jacobites were drawn, with the Whig government of Walpole; and in Scotland, there was continuing unease at the realities of Union, highlighted by disaffection among the lairds at the lack of political preferment, by unrest in Glasgow and Edinburgh in 1725 and 1736, and by the privations of near-famine in the Highlands. After a plan to land an army on one flank, near London, had come to nothing in 1744, the 24-year-old Charles took another course in July 1745, sailing from the Loire and Brest with two ships bound for thc Outer Hebrides.

Word from Scotland had been that 6,000 French troops, arms for 10,000 others and finance to the tune of 30,000 louis-d'or was the minimum required, but Charles had only a seventh of this sum, a sizeable stock of arms and ammunition and one company of French volunteer officers on sailing – and on landfall rather less, having lost *L'Elisabeth*, savaged in an encounter with an English gunship *en route*. Small wonder that the key Jacobites of Skye – MacDonald of Sleat and MacLeod of MacLeod – refused to join him. Small wonder that even aboard *Le du Teillay* opinion was divided. That Charles himself nevertheless landed near Arisaig on 11 August is testimony to his courage, or brazenness, or irresponsibility.

Having met with some ill-luck hitherto, Charles was then attended by almost unrelenting good fortune. Firstly, some local clans did join him – notably that of Lochiel – so that on 19 August he was able to raise the Jacobite standard at Glenfinnan amidst some 1,200 men, with more under way. Then, General Cope, charged with resisting the rebellion but abandoned by the Scottish whigs, saw fit to march first to Inverness, leaving the way to Edinburgh virtually open to a rebel army which by Perth had been strengthened by the advent of Lord George Murray and by Edinburgh had swelled to some 2,500 or more. And on shipping back to Dunbar via Aberdeen, Cope then allowed his little-trained force to be surprised at Prestonpans in a dawn attack on 21 September by a Jacobite army, which, despite irregular weaponry, put in a formidable charge. Eye-witnesses claim that 'in less than five minutes we obtained a complete victory, with a terrible carnage on the part of the enemy' (Chevalier de Johnstone, 27), that 'the whole prospect was filled with runaways, and Highlanders pursuing them' (A. Carlyle, 414), and that 'Noses, Hands, Arms, Legs were promiscuously to be seen in some Places of the Field' (anon).

Were Charles's launching of the Rising not his greatest error, then that came now. As many contemporary pundits remarked: 'had the Rebels, flush'd with victory follow'd their Blow, whilst the Hearts of his Majesty's Subjects were dismay'd by General Cope's Defeat, and very few disciplin'd Troops in England, it is hard to say what would have been the Consequence' (Ray, 56). Instead, Charles tarried some six weeks in Edinburgh, hoping against hope for French reinforcements, before marching on England on 1 November. Carlisle fell and again resistance was slight, but equally slight was support from the English Jacobites – support which Charles had promised to the still-sceptical chiefs. It was a march remarkable for its swiftness, for the abandoned villages it passed through, for its discipline belying reports of pillage, and for its end.

At Derby a hotly fought council of war was held, the chiefs proposing – so Lord Elcho subsequently reported – that 'they had marched far enough into England, and as they had received not the least Encouragement from any person of distinction, the French not landed, and only joined by 200 vagabonds, they had done their part' (427). In addition, English armies were closing. To Charles's chagrin, on 5 December – with London in panic – the decision was taken to turn back.

Winter conditions were severe – one of their pursuers writes of 'a terrible hard and cold Gale of Wind, which nips our Noses and Ears in a most piercing Manner' (Volunteer, 33) – yet even in retreat the army acquitted itself remarkably well, getting the better of a skirmish at Clifton, making Hamilton and Glasgow by Christmas, and routing a government force at Falkirk on 17 January 1746.

But with Cumberland nearing and making Aberdeen by March, things were taking their final turn. The highland army was ill-fed and pay was running out: Cumberland's forces might be 'most extream ill' (Volunteer, 122), but they were superior in training, in experience, in fire-power and in sheer numbers. Charles's decision not to take to the Highlands to regroup for a guerilla campaign, but to face Cumberland on the grotesquely ill-chosen Culloden Moor signed the death warrant of his enterprise and of some 1,000 of his devoted followers, fighting as they were 'prodigiously tired by hunger and fatigue' (Elcho, 433). Culloden was as decisive for the government as Prestonpans had been for Charles. Walking sword in hand and wigless through the rioters and squibs of the London streets after the news came in, Smollett remarked, 'John Bull is as haughty and valiant tonight as he was abject and cowardly on the Black Wednesday, when the Highlanders were at Derby' (A. Carlyle, 416–17).

And Culloden's aftermath was no less ruthless. The Prince himself, hunted over the Highlands and Islands with £30,000 on his head, did finally get a boat to France in September 1746. Many of his followers were less fortunate: the wounded were either butchered on the battlefield or hounded as they fled, Cumberland cutting through their lands a swathe of pillage, rape, murder and fire. Reports are contradictory and records far from complete – especially on the lower ranks and on those who did not survive – but of those 'out' in the Forty-five, some thousand were killed in battle, the vast majority of them at Culloden, some 130 executed, some 660 transported.

The government then set out to deal a death blow to the Gaelic culture of the Highlands, proscribing its language and dress from 1747. Attempts to establish English colonies in the glens met with less than success, but the Anglicization of Scotland took its course. By 1749 Prestonpans had become the site of a sulphuric acid works; by the mid-1750s the Duke of Cumberland had become Rector of St Andrews University.

17 The silences of *Waverley*

'And what is your edition of the story, sir?'

Guy Mannering, XI

In a disparaging notice on *Waverley* in late 1814, *The Critical Review* remarked that 'the main incidents are merely the rebellion of 1745, treated "novelwise"'. One has only to compare the above with the plot of the novel, however, to discover that this is by no means the case. On the contrary, *Waverley* is notable for what it leaves out.

That may seem an unhelpful remark: after all, all history is an account of the past and could not be an *account* of the past if it did not leave out some of the past. *Waverley*, however, leaves out virtually all of the Rising after Clifton, indeed makes almost no mention of the Battle of Culloden and its aftermath, nor any whatsoever of the Prince in the heather. Even the Fortinbras of the affair, the Duke of Cumberland – about whom in 1745 there was little bonnie – is scarcely mentioned, entering the novel not at all. Nor is the Rising before Clifton treated in balanced circumstantial detail: there is no coverage of the movements of the Prince before Edinburgh, nor any really detailed account of the march south. A more appropriate verdict on Scott might thus be that of the *Scots Magazine* of 1814: 'we feel some wish that he had carried us through the whole series of the rebellion'.

It is useful to have these omissions clearly in mind – not least because the novel is often misrepresented. In two of the best recent books on Scott, for example, one can still find claims that Edward witnesses the battle of Falkirk (Brown, 21) or that Scott lingers over the march into England (Kerr, 33), when in each case it is Prestonpans which is being described. Worse, one of Europe's best-known literary encyclopaedias, *Kindler*, states that Edward is *captured* at *Culloden*!

More important, however, is that in literary terms – especially in terms of the genre-to-be, the early historical novel – these omissions are remarkable: imagine what a Tolstoy would have made of the discussions on *Le du Teillay*, an Erckmann-Chatrian of the long march south, a Thackeray of the council of war at Derby, a Pérez Galdós of Culloden, a Balzac or Pushkin of the depredations afterwards, a Stevenson of the Prince in the heather.

The omission of Culloden is no less remarkable, however, in terms of Scott's own convictions stated elsewhere. In an important piece on the *Culloden Papers* for the *Quarterly Review* of January 1816, Scott writes of 'the severities exercised with a most unsparing hand, after the insurrection of 1745, during the course of which the highlanders had conducted themselves with humanity and moderation' (*CP* 330). Such attitudes enter his fiction too, *The Highland Widow* recording 'the sense of general indignation entertained, not unjustly, through the Highlands of Scotland, on account of the barbarous and violent conduct of the victors after the battle of Culloden' (*HW* 3).

The question arises, therefore, why Scott's version of Forty-fiving should omit so much. One inescapable conclusion is that of Duncan Forbes, who argues that '*Waverley* was not intended to be a "story about the '45"' its emphasis being rather on recording states of society which the Rising brought into open conflict (31). Given, however, that Scott *does* portray part of the Rising in detail, it is difficult not to conclude also that the *silence du texte* over Culloden is eloquent of a wish not to embarrass the forces of political union.

18 The turn from 'drum and trumpet' history

the ferocious warrior is remembered, and the peaceful abbots are abandoned to forgetfulness and oblivion *The Antiquary*, XVII

Yet to insist on what *Waverley* omits is to do it far less than justice: in historical terms, the work is far more striking for what it includes – a fact perhaps best brought out by comparison with the former historiography of the Forty-five.

To say that Scott was well versed in this early historiography would be an understatement: his accounts of Prestonpans and Clifton, he records in the final chapter, are 'taken from the narrative of intelligent eye-witnesses, and corrected from the *History of the Rebellion* by the late venerable author of *Douglas*' (341), and his library contains not only the latter – John Home's *The History of the Rebellion in the Year 1745* (1802) – but also a host of works which could be meant by the former, including those of Michael Hughes, the Chevalier de Johnstone, James Macpherson, and James Ray. In addition, the library has a prodigious and invaluable assemblage of documents on the Forty-five, ranging from histories to homilies, from treatises to travelogues, from proclamations to poems, from sermons to songs, to journals, letters, newspapers, odes, pamphlets, prints and dying speeches – all in all, some 250 items, varying in length from the fly-sheet to the fully-fledged volume. There is no richer museum of Forty-five-iana than Abbotsford – and its owner-curator was not loath to express his opinions on the quality of individual items.

Conventional wisdom, founded on Scott's own statement, is that the major sources of *Waverley* are Home, Ray and Johnstone. Writing of Home's work in 1827, however, and commenting on the fact that it is dedicated to George III, Scott says bluntly 'Mr Home ought either never to have written his history, or to have written it without clogging himself with the dedication to the sovereign' (*JH* 207). Referring to Johnstone in the same review, Scott grants that he 'has made better professional remarks on the Highland mode of fighting, and mere tactics, than we have observed in any other work' but states that he 'wrote under the influence of disappointment and ill-humour' and was 'somewhat of a gasconader' (*JH* 211). And as for Ray's *Compleat History of the Rebellion* (1754), Scott has, as he occasionally did, penned a terse comment on the inside pages of his own edition, writing on one page the word 'Curious' and on another: 'The writer may be trusted in what he says he saw allowing for party heat and violence but his information from report is terribly inaccurate.'

Such criticisms demonstrate that Scott was very much the inquiring historian, on his guard both against what in *The Antiquary* he calls 'the idle jade Rumour' (*TA* 38) and against bias. The wavering stance of his hero is guard against the latter, the role allotted in the plot to misconstruction a warning against the former. But Scott's greatest criticism of his sources lies in the overall temporal structure he develops for his Forty-five – a structure which gives the reader a very different perspective on the Rising.

Consider his most substantial and recent predecessor, Home. This 350-page history is certainly a considerable temporal structure, its duration extending from the Fifteen to the flight of the Prince and its geographical scope stretching to include events on the European mainland. Within this broad canvas, however, Home's criteria for relevance to Forty-fiving are rigid indeed. Some 90 per cent of the text is 'drum and trumpet' history, devoted to the movements of armies; yet scarcely any figure beneath commander is named, battles are portrayed as manoeuvres leading to casualties and the depredations of war are scarcely touched on, except briefly in Edinburgh. The result is that one can read the book from end to end without gaining any clear picture of why the Rising took place, why it failed, what it was like to live through and what its effects were.

Than this, *Waverley* could scarcely be more different: only about one-tenth of its narrative is spent on the battlefield or march and almost none in the counsel chamber – and the cast is spread accordingly. Here Forty-fiving is a far more social and domestic affair, affecting far more of society.

History is a study of causes: the job of the historian, writes E.H. Carr is to assemble 'more and more answers to the question, "Why?"' (89). In evolving a temporal structure which includes the state of the Highlands, the mood of the Lowlands, the temper of the English Country faction around Edward's uncle and the high-handedness and corruption of the Walpole administration around Edward's father, Scott is offering a much fuller explanation for the Forty-five than many a blow-by-blow account.

The historical achievement of *Waverley* is to present a far broader field of perceived relevance. In a great act of colligation, Scott brings together the insights of *philosophie de l'histoire* and the human detail of a huge mass of documentation scrutinized with the methods of emergent history to produce a new vision of the past. As Macaulay wrote in 1828: 'Sir Walter Scott ... has used those fragments of truth which historians have scornfully thrown behind them in a manner which may well excite their envy. He has constructed out of their gleanings works which, even considered as histories, are scarcely less valuable than their's' (278). The result is a decisive turn from the history of the battlefield and cabinet room to the history of the people.

19 The civilian on the battlefield

For War a new and dreadful language spoke,
  Never by ancient warrior heard or known
The Vision of Don Roderick, XXVI

This shift in historical emphasis is perhaps best demonstrated at the place it might seem least likely to emerge – the battlefield at Prestonpans. Consider Scott's account in chapter II, 24 in comparison with the three contemporary versions from Scott's collection – two Hanoverian (A, B) and one Jacobite (C) – printed in the appendix.

Scott's account and theirs are by no means totally dissimilar: the same outcome – a Hanoverian rout – is attributed to the same overall causes – surprise and indiscipline – and all four writers apportion blame or praise accordingly. The detail and very wording of the clansmen's bare-headed prayer before battle suggest that Scott has in fact used the *Caledonian Mercury* as a source.

A whole series of differences, however, demonstrate that Scott's has been no scissors-and-paste approach. His account is far less partisan, with neither the detraction from the clans' achievement found in B, nor its adulation as in C, and when it comes to controversies – did Charles send for surgeons, or did he, as some reports state, breakfast within sound of the wounded and dying? – Scott is discreetly silent.

More importantly, because of the prior knowledge he has given us of the clans – including the magnificent description of their forces in II, 21 – and thanks to the rich circumstantiality of his narrative, his battle is not a bald 'short Dispute' as in A, nor an affair turning upon the unexplained 'Manner of the *Highlander*'s Behaviour in the Attack' as in B, but an event which achieves that condition of good history: followability.

Above all, however, his Prestonpans is a more personal and personalized affair. He is the only author to name soldiers below the rank of commander, the only one to hint at the human motives of the actors involved, and the only one to portray what it feels like to be involved in such an encounter:

Waverley felt his heart at that moment throb as it would have burst from his bosom. It was not fear, it was not ardour, – it was a compound of both, a new and deeply energetic impulse, that with its first emotion chilled and astounded, then fevered and maddened his mind. The sounds around him combined to exalt his enthusiasm; the pipes played, and the clans rushed forward, each in its own dark column. (225)

Whilst in C 'Courage and Ardour' are taken as given, they are here submitted to scrutiny. And whereas in C, B and especially A, the conflict is just a prelude to ascertaining losses, securing hardware and re-grouping, it is here embedded in Edward's overall learning process. One of his conversations with Talbot hinges on precisely this experience:

'Fighting! pooh, what have you seen but a skirmish or two? – Ah! if you saw war on the grand scale – sixty or a hundred thousand men in the field on each side.'

'I am not at all curious, Colonel, – Enough, says our homely proverb is as good as a feast. The plumed troops and the big war used to enchant me in poetry, but the night marches, vigils, couches under the winter sky, and such accompaniments of the glorious trade, are not at all to my taste in practice; – then for dry blows, I had *my* fill of fighting at Clifton, where I escaped by a hair's breadth half a dozen times, and you, I should think' – He stopped.

'Had enough at Preston? you mean to say,' said the Colonel, laughing; 'but 'tis my vocation, Hal.'

'It is not mine though,' said Waverley; 'and having honourably got rid of the sword which I drew only as a volunteer, I am quite satisfied with my military experience, and shall be in no hurry to take it up again.' (290–1)

The verdict on military matters is pointed – as is again the difference between Edward the learner and Talbot the old dog – but equally pointed is the verdict on the way such matters have been portrayed in poetry.

Writing of Scott's scenes of military violence, Daiches has argued that 'Nowhere in literature is there a more vivid presentation of the cruel senselessness of war', adding: 'It is all, in fact, in *Waverley*' (1971, 63). That is perhaps an overstatement, and one unjust to the achievement in this area of Tolstoy, Erckmann-Chatrian and Pérez Galdós, not to mention the war novels of our own century. But it is this tradition that *Waverley* inaugurates. Edward is not a civilian but a neophyte officer little suited to military life; nevertheless, his experiences at Prestonpans usher in what will become a major topos in the historical fiction of the nineteenth-century and beyond – the civilian on the battlefield.

Just compare Edward with his renowned literary successor, Fabrice del Dongo, who stumbles in increasing shock and incredulity across the battlefield at Waterloo in Stendhal's *The Charterhouse of Parma* (1839). Both are young men, fresh from private education. Both have read especially history, historical epic and chivalric romance. And both find that their reading has left them quite unprepared for the new social realities they encounter. But the crisis of expectation is the dawn of understanding – and the historical novel is the genre written about and for their mutual embarrassment. It is the new history – the new followability – for an age of such exponential change that the old histories are leaving it in the lurch.

20 The eclipse of epic and ballad

> the young women wanted pins, ribbons, combs, and ballads
>
> *Guy Mannering*, VI

If in terms of history such passages are a turn from 'drum and trumpet' accounts, in terms of literature they are a turn from the epic and ballad.

The ballad, recent critics tell us, is one of those genres whose prime function is to remember: to remember kings, tribes, traditions and the deeds of heroes. The ballad, in other words, is a particular temporal structure corresponding to a particular version of the past: 'In such a context', the French novelist Michel Butor remarks in 'Individu et groupe dans le roman' (1964), 'the history of a country will be the history of its kings, the tale of war, the tale of the exploits of its great captains'.

Now that is just the context portrayed by Scott in his early poetry, which appropriately adopts the form of the lay or ballad for its portrayal. In *The Lay of the Last Minstrel*, he depicts the bards as 'The jovial priests of mirth and war; / Alike for feast and fight prepared' (VI, 3), and after the success of that work can marvel in *Marmion* at 'How still the legendary lay / O'er poet's bosom holds its sway / How on the ancient minstrel strain / time lays his palsied hand in vain' (Intro. I). In the mature Scott, however, time's hand is never infirm, and having portrayed the modern balladeers in *Don Roderick* as 'weak minstrels of a laggard lay' (Intro.), he bids his final valedictory to minstrelsy in *The Lord of the Isles*, portraying himself as

> – a lonely gleaner I,
> Through fields time-wasted, on sad inquest bound
> Where happier bards of yore have richer harvest found. (I)

The figure of Mac-Murrough nan Fion in *Waverley* is part of that sad inquest. Living in his own bard's croft and in the pay and favour of Fergus, Mac-Murrough is precisely a poet of remembrance: even Sassenach Edward can grasp that the stirring piece declaimed at the feast seems to 'recite many proper names, to lament the dead, to apostrophize the absent, to exhort and entreat and animate those who were present' (98). Flora thus characterizes the *bhairds* as 'poets and historians of their tribes' (103). Persist though this oral culture might at Glennaquoich, however, the aged Mac-Murrough and his genre are seen throughout as doomed to decay: for Flora, the bards' craft is already a subject of study (101), and while Fergus may rate Mac-Murrough above Homer, her own verdict is somewhat less flattering (103).

The cause of this decline, Scott suggests, is an inherent obsolescence. One of Fergus's frets is to have 'a bard to sing of deeds which he dare not imitate' (103), and when he does seek to put them into practice it costs him his life. The vision of the past evoked by the temporal structure of the ballad is no longer in step with the march of society. When in Scott's later novels – as in *Guy Mannering* – the ballad enters the plot, it is as part of a mid-eighteenth-century upbringing, but not as a manner of life.

And as ballad, so epic. A feature of *Waverley*, noted by the earliest reviewers is its 'aptitude for classical comment and quotation' (*The Scourge*) – notably from Virgil's *Aeneid*. Some of this is just a mark of a character's education or pomposity, but elsewhere more is at stake. When Fergus aptly cites Virgil's epic before his execution this is perhaps also a comment on the inaptness of the epic-like undertaking he has himself risked in an age when the time for epics is long past. Much the same could be said of Bradwardine's much-cited remark on his own demise 'To be sure we may say with Virgilius Maro, *Fuimus Troes* – and there's the end of an old song' (303): 'the end of an old song' is a lovely colloquial rendering of the Latin, an ironic reference to James Ogilvy's famous remark on signing the Union treaty in 1707, but perhaps also a hint that the old song of the epic is being replaced by the 'bourgeois epic' of the novel.

Such passages of what we would now call 'intertextuality' show that not only is Edward an avid reader trying to orient himself in life: Scott too is a (far more) avid reader anxious to mark off his portrayal of the past from that of earlier literature. As Carlyle saw, Scott was 'among the first to perceive that the day of Metrical Chivalry Romances was declining' (Hayden, 360–1). In *Waverley* begins a tradition – carried forward by Stendhal, Tolstoy and Fontane – in which the historical novel distances itself from the epic and ballad and sets out its new terms for narrating *arma virumque*.

21 Historical romance: a new use of the past

that particular class of compositions which hovers between romance and history *Lives of the Novelists*: 'Daniel Defoe'

Scott's new form of narrative, the historical romance, is characterized, however, not only by the broader temporal structure and more minutely discriminated time-scale described above but also by a mixing of the verified and the unverified, which greatly complicates its relationship to history.

This *mélange* permeates the entire text. Not only are there verified events – Prestonpans and Clifton – side by side with non-verified – Cairnvreckan and Ullswater; not only are there verified persons – the Prince and Gardner – side by side with non-verified – Edward and Evan Dhu; even within the verified there is the unverified – as when Gardner dying from many wounds at Prestonpans (vouchsafed) casts an unattested dying glance at Edward. And as Scott's closest scrutinizers on this issue – James Anderson and *Waverley*'s pre-eminent editor, Claire Lamont – have shown, the mixing goes further: on the one hand, there is a host of details which Scott has derived from his copious source material, while on the other, the hunting party launching the Rising and several military details have been imported from the Fifteen. This is not quite the same blend as in the documentary novel or 'faction': it is a particular type of Romantic literary 'coagination'.

Nor, of course, is it the 'colligation' of the historian. The difference between historical romance and history lies in a different response to one of the fundamental problems of history: not knowing. Historians often don't know and sometimes don't know what they don't know. In such a situation, they can either be silent themselves or can use what is one of the most intriguing parts of their method – the argument from silence. What they cannot do is what Scott here does: assume authorial omniscience. The historian may sometimes rely on conceptual evidence to produce an acceptable narrative: he cannot do that as often as Scott does here. A fictional narrative is one which relies wholly on conceptual evidence – as Scott does with Fergus. Fergus acts as a Jacobite leader *could have* acted. For the historian 'could have' is not enough. History attempts to give the past *wie es eigentlich gewesen* or as evidence forces it to believe it was: historical romance enacts a *possibility* within a given and fixed past.

From the first, objections to this new composite have been raised, a typical response being that of the *Quarterly Review* for July 1814: 'We confess that we have, speaking generally, a great objection to what may be called historical romance, in which real and fictitious personages, and actual and fabulous events are mixed together to the utter confusion of the reader, and the unsettling of all accurate recollections of past transactions.'

This reaction is in part justified and important. However much Scott insists that 'It is not our intention to intrude upon the province of history' (263), *Waverley* inevitably does: from the outset historians have taken issue with its favourable portrayal of the Prince and its less favourable of the Jacobites. It is not a tautology to say that histories of the Forty-five written post-1814 are written after *Waverley*. And in such a context it is essential that a blend does not become a blur, that the cocktail ingredients, romance and history, are kept apart.

On the other hand, it is essential also to recognize that this is something Scott repeatedly does himself in footnotes and prefaces added to later editions. Moreover, most early critics had no difficulty in dealing with Scott's form – which was then taken up by major realist writers right across Europe, became one of the most practised and most read genres of the nineteenth century and is now part of our critical idiom. One must not forget that, as J.H. Plumb has written, 'The more literate and sophisticated the society becomes, the more complex and powerful become the uses to which the past is put' (11). *Waverley* is one of these complex uses of the past, complex in being not only an implicit critique of the – far less sophisticated – history of its own day and hence a stimulus to future historians, but also a literary exploration both of a specific past and of the increasingly troubled relationship between our presents and the pasts we are leaving behind. To approach *Waverley* with purely historical criteria is unliterary: to approach it with only the criteria of modern history is unhistorical as well.

22 Metahistory: the historians in the historical novel

'I repeat the little history now, as I have a hundred times done before, merely because I would wring some sense out of it.'

Redgauntlet, Letter I

Waverley, however, is not only itself a sophisticated use of the past, but also a study of a society in which the past is already put to sophisticated uses. This is reflected in a feature of the cast destined to have a great impact on historical fiction: the historians in the historical novel.

In *Waverley*, these figures stand out for their sheer number. Not only Mr Pembroke, whose two volumes of history are 'the labour of the worthy man's whole life' (28) or Mac-Murrough, whose life is likewise devoted to recalling things past, not only Bradwardine, steeped in things antiquarian and Edward steeped in historical reading, but Flora with her poem on Captain Wogan, Rose with 'several heavy tomes of history' (64) on her syllabus, and Edward's uncle, regaling his nephew with 'family tradition and genealogical history' (16) – all are indicative of a society under the sway of *historia magistra vitae.* Sir Herbert Butterfield has written: 'It would seem that the decline of religion gives undue power to history in the shaping of men's minds – undue power to historical over-simplifications' (30). Be that as it may, in Scott's account of the Forty-five – which was in part a confessional rebellion – it is striking how little the old master-narrative of religion is invoked: in his Forty-five, the Book of Books is being supplanted by the Book of the Past.

Politically, his Forty-five is a struggle not only for Britain's future but for its past, a contest between different ways of remembering and different ideas of what is to be remembered: Pembroke's tomes, Mac-Murrough's recitations, Flora's poem, even the notorious 'lang pedigree' of regal portraits beneath which Edward waits to meet the Prince at Holyrood House (191) – each of these is a 'practical past' (Oakeshott, 103), a history created to serve political ends. The consequences for Edward when his two-volume Pembroke or even Flora's poem fall into Hanoverian hands is a literary anticipation of what the sociologists now tell us: 'images of the past commonly legitimate a present social order. It is an implicit rule that participants in any social order must presuppose a shared memory' (Connerton, 3).

As often in historical fiction, however, a political theme is mirrored on the personal plane. All around, characters are formulating narratives to make their own lives intelligible or tolerable, be it Edward's uncle and aunt, regaling him with the 'oft-repeated tale of narrative old age' (15), Humphrey Houghton's parents refusing to believe 'that their son fell otherwise than fighting by the young squire's side' (331), or Alick, another Waverley retainer, telling 'a liberal allowance of desperate battles, grisly executions, and raw-head and bloody-bone stories' (331) on his return home. They and others embody an insight upheld by modern philosophy, that 'man is in his actions and practice, as well as in his fictions, essentially a story-telling animal' (MacIntyre, 216). Not each of us is a Wandering Willie, but we all need stories to parse our lives.

The prime example of this is Edward himself. He is not, admittedly, like many a Scott protagonist – Guy Mannering, Lovell in *The Antiquary*, or Darsie Latimer in *Redgauntlet* – a lost heir in search of the missing account which will render his life narratable and hence intelligible and hence bearable. He is in search not of an account but of a way of accounting – and finds it in his shift of mode from romance to real history. For *each* of these is of course a narrative structure, a making. As Kerr, in the best study of this aspect of *Waverley* has written, 'The "real history" of Waverley's life has for Scott the same fictive status as its "romance" ' (18).

The figure, however, who most memorably unites the uses and abuses of history in his person is the Baron of Bradwardine. Abstracted in his studies, a stickler for ritual, well into his anecdotage and a pedant of unending *minutiae*, the Baron is Scott's first antiquarian. As historian, he 'only cumbered his memory with matters of fact; the cold, dry, hard outlines which history delineates' – whereas Edward 'loved to fill up and round the sketch with the colouring of a warm and vivid imagination, which gives light and life to the actors and speakers in the drama of past ages' (57). Like his renowned successor, Oldbuck in *The Antiquary*, the Baron is thus the historical novel's *apologia*, the novel playing Edward/Edie to the Bradwardine/Oldbuck of conventional history. But the Baron is more. The stories he uses to parse his life may be the classics, but they make him one of the most admirable combatants in the Rising, unswerving in honour and nobly stoic in defeat. His insistence, after Prestonpans, on the ritual of untying the Prince's brogue may be the epitome of the untimely, embarrassing to the Chevalier, and ludicrously feudal even to Fergus, yet it is also a reinstatement of performative memory to which Scott and Edward are not wholly unsympathetic. It is an attempt to do something close to the novel's heart – to keep open the communications with a fast-retreating past.

One should not overstate these metahistorical elements: *Waverley* is not *The Antiquary*, which goes farther in this area, nor *Redgauntlet*, which goes farther again; and Scott is not Tolstoy. Nevertheless, part of the stature of *Waverley* is that, itself a representation of the past, it is a novel about the role of such representations in society and personal life. It is a fitting end to such a novel that Edward should ask Farmer Jopson 'carefully to preserve for him his Highland garb and accoutrements, particularly the arms, curious in themselves' (292) and that the restored Tully-Veolan should be adorned with a painting of Edward and Fergus in highland dress, the clan in the background (338). In this historical novel, this verbal museum, the highland culture is itself finally given museum status.

Chapter 4

Waverley as initiator

23 The novelty of Scott's historical novel

Which I was born to introduce... *Journal*, 17 October 1826

'No-one ever begins.' Alexis's remark, made in his obituary of Scott in 1832, is an appropriate *caveat* to this chapter. Of course, *Waverley* has its debts to predecessors, but do these debts mean that Scott's historical novel as form has no credit left, no novelty to call its own?

There are those who would limit or annul any suggestion of radical novelty in *Waverley* by placing it within one of two larger traditions. George Watson has described the historical novel as an 'expanding form from Mme de Lafayette's *La Princesse de Clèves* (1678) to Scott's *Waverley*' (156) – a tendency George Saintsbury had already taken to its logical conclusion with the remark, 'Who wrote the first Historical Novel? The orthodox, and perhaps on the whole the sufficient, answer to this is, Xenophon.' And similarly, other critics, including Lukács, have seen the historical novel as just another facet of the novel at large and not constituting a genre in its own right at all.

There is *prima facie* evidence both for and against such arguments. On the one hand, the term 'historical novel' is certainly older than *Waverley* and some forty years older than its earliest *OED* entry: it appears on the title pages of works of fiction (by Mrs E.M. Foster and anon.) as long before as 1795 and 1787, and by 1814 Mrs Byron and Jane West also had 'historical novels' to their names. Equally, as Scott's opening chapter and later prefaces in part make clear, *Waverley* is in debt to earlier fiction for both structure and theme – to the Gothic novel for its journey and past locus, to the regional novel *à la* Maria Edgeworth for its location on the edge and interest in national character, to the social novel for its minutely discriminated time-scale. On the other hand, critics in Scott's lifetime were struck less by his debts to others than by those of others to him: in 1814 the *Monthly Review* argued that *Waverley* 'is strictly an historical romance and yet scarcely belongs to any class of composition usually decorated with that title', while in 1832 *The Day* wrote that 'Sir Walter Scott, while by his own writings he created a European reputation, has, in fact, also created everywhere a new school of novel, tale, and romance composition.' Similarly, John Dunlop's *The History of Fiction*, published in 1814, makes no mention of historical fiction in Britain – a fact all the more telling in that it does find 'historical novels' in the French tradition and traces historical romance there back to 1517.

Given the inconclusiveness of such extrinsic evidence, one must turn to the intrinsic – and here two striking novelties in Scott become apparent. Firstly, *Waverley* is about not just the past but the pastness of the past, about a past which is qualitatively different from the present. This leads to its paradoxical temporal duality: it portrays the past both at no remove and at a distance, both 'as it actually happens' to Edward and 'as it actually happened' in the eyes of Scott the historian, as if Scott could both be moved to portray the Forty-five and forget whatever had moved him – a tension which leads to several other topoi. And secondly, this and other features are allowed all the more play in that *Waverley* has the unprecedented breadth detailed above – what Ruskin called 'Scott's larger view of human life' (Hayden, 525). The panorama of an age, the broad cast, the turn to social history; the far-flung spot, the backward culture, the simultaneity of the non-simultaneous; the journey, the go-between, the assessment of both sides; the fictive characters among the verified, the meeting with the leader, the questioning of the Great Man; the realism of rebellion, the civilian on the battlefield, war 'coming home' to the populace; the historian-figures, the reflections on history, the valedictory to the epic; the themes of change and stasis, centralism and nationhood, cultural tolerance – all these are both part and parcel of *Waverley* and the stock-in-trade of the subsequent genre.

From the above intrinsic evidence three conclusions for the historical novel as genre ensue. Firstly, the many definitions of the historical novel as a novel set 'in an historical period', set 'half a century back', set 'in an age in which the writer did not live' are all inadequate since they fail to distinguish between a novel such as *Waverley* set in a past past, understood as different from the present, and the myriad earlier works set in a past understood as no different from the present. Further, any insistence that an historical novel 'contain at least one historical personage' is open to the objection that one of the aims of early historical fiction is to re-assess just what constitutes such a person. Indeed, thirdly, any definition of an historical novel as containing feature *x* or *y* or features *x* and *y* is – however handy for delimiting a particular inquiry – liable to be either arbitrary or less than helpful. (Such definitions tend to reduce the argument to the bald 'an historical novel is a novel that is historical'.) More useful in this particular case is to say that an historical novel is one which shares enough of the above family resemblances (and of any others introduced by subsequent family members and branches) for it to make sense for us to describe it as one of the family. There need be no resemblance present in all members, nor any one member who has all resemblances, but the family must be recognizable as such.

And as such it has traced and will trace its family tree back not to Xenophon or Mrs Foster or Maria Edgeworth but to Scott. Beginnings are in part determined by followers, and it was from Scott that the many followers began. 'No-one ever begins' – but of all the new departures in the past of literature few can have been so signally and successfully instigated by one writer.

24 *Waverley* and the Waverley Novels

... Refined it first and showed its use

Journal, 17 October 1826

It is often believed, however, that having introduced the historical novel, Scott did not refine but just repeated it: 'To describe *Waverley*', claims an influential modern study, 'is indeed to describe many of Scott's twenty-six novels' (Cusac,

27). That Scott's plotting has a crackable code is an idea as old as the 1820s and an assessment of it is a precondition to an assessment of *Waverley*'s first impact – on Scott himself.

Comparing *Waverley* with the Waverley Novels, Cusac finds that 'there is a serious conflict involving more than the confrontation of two characters, an important structural element which is found in twenty-one of the novels'. Further, 'There is a journey, found in fourteen. There is the contrast of cultures, which figures importantly in twenty. There are two heroines, found in four. There is an uncle-nephew relationship, present in ten.' And '*Waverley* is a story of initiation, as are five others' (27). But such similarities are as inconclusive as they are incontrovertible, since they are the type of similarity in and around which manifold differences can thrive.

Even if one restricts oneself to the Scottish novels, one finds marked differences in narrator, structure and subject-matter – narrators ranging from the omniscient of *Waverley*, to the first-person of *Rob Roy*, the epistolary of *Redgauntlet* and the framework story-teller of *Tales of My Landlord*, first series; structures ranging from full-blown (at times over-blown) novels such as *The Pirate* to short tales such *The Two Drovers*; and subject-matter ranging forward to contemporary, 'new-fangled' Scotland in *St Ronan's Well*, and back via the Fifteen in *Rob Roy* and the post-Union and pre-Union periods of *The Black Dwarf* and *The Bride of Lammermoor*, to the Middle Ages in *The Fair Maid of Perth*. Such ranging is not incidental to the genre: it brings a further harvest of topoi and themes. Among the topoi to prove seminal are the improver, the outlaw figure, the spy, the astrologer, the prediction, and above all the crowd scenes of *The Heart of Midlothian*, while thematically these novels bring not only a deepening of the themes of nationhood, Union, revolution and heroism, but also new issues such as religious tolerance and *plus ça change*, and in *Redgauntlet* history as self-discovery and self-healing.

For sure, these novels also show what Cusac and many others have pointed out: that the *Waverley* model opens many more windows on the past than just those onto the Forty-five. For sure, there is repetition here – as in every other prolific

European realist from Balzac to Fontane. But what is also striking is how, even in illness and debt, Scott has an eye to his imitators, considering 'like a fox at his last shifts whether there be a way to dodge them' (*J*, 215), and how much of the later genre his shifts anticipate. It is not an irony to argue that perhaps Scott's greatest and most influential influence was on his own Waverley Novels. As *The Scotsman* wrote in 1832, Scott was not only a 'Columbus of fiction' but, 'more fortunate than the discoverer of the New World, he was destined to explore almost every corner of the extensive territory which he had the merit of first making known to his countrymen'.

25 The influence on the early European historical novel

I am something like Captain Bobadil who trained up a hundred gentlemen to fight very nearly if not altogether as well as myself.

Journal, 17 October 1826

Given *Waverley*'s influence on the Waverley Novels, and given their influence across Europe and beyond, it is impossible to mark where its influence ends and theirs begins. Nevertheless, it can be demonstrated that *Waverley* had a marked European influence, and to compare it with the works it influenced is to shed light on both them and it.

The impact of *Waverley* in Europe preceded its translation: of key figures in its influence, Stendhal had read it by May 1815, Tieck claims to have brought the first copy to Germany in July 1817 and Menzel's alert *Literaturblatt* notices it and its successors in the same year. Nevertheless, the vogue for Scott did depend in good measure on his translatability – as *The Day* wrote in January 1832, 'the curse of Babel proves only a momentary obstacle to the diffusion of such genius and talent as he possesses' – and close analysis and imitation of *Waverley* came only after translation. It was not always the first of Scott's novels to be translated: that was often *Guy Mannering*. Nor was it the most popular, which was *Ivanhoe*. It had, however, been translated into at least seven European languages by 1827, the earliest being French (1818) and German (1821–2) and the last, Russian – with German having two rival translations, *Waverley* and *Eduard*. Of other central figures in the early European historical novel, Victor Hugo was reviewing Scott by 1819, Mérimée reading him assiduously that same year, Alexis writing incisively on him by 1823, Pushkin steeped in him by 1825 and Gogol following suit soon after. Shortly before Scott's death, Washington Irving wrote from Europe that 'Of living writers I should say that Walter Scott is the only one that has a reputation sufficient to make himself known in most towns' and in 1835 there were no doubt many who could have echoed Pushkin's letter to his Natalia, 'I am reading Walter Scott's novels, which I am in rapture over, and I am moaning for you.'

Writing in the mid-1830s of issues neglected by Russian periodicals, Gogol listed first 'What was Walter Scott and how is his influence to be understood?' Of Scott novels in general it could be said that their broader canvases matched the wider horizons of the Europe of the 1820s and 1830s, their museum impulse, the losses due to exponential change. *Waverley* itself, however, had a specific appeal: its theme of rebellion. This was the Europe which Metternich described as seething with insurrection, and countless historical novels, tales and *Novellen* took up the theme – the rising of the French Camisards proving a favourite instance. The minatory note of Scott's words, 'Let us devoutly hope, that, in this respect at least, we shall never see the scenes, or hold the sentiments, that were general in Britain Sixty Years since' (319) struck a chord around Europe.

An early example of such novels is *The Uprising in the Cevennes* (1826) by Ludwig Tieck. Replace Edward by Edmund, replace the Highlands of 1745 by the Cevennes of 1703, replace the highland Jacobites by the Camisards, replace the Hanoverian forces by the troops of the French king – and you have much of Tieck cut and dried. Similarly unabashed in its derivation from *Waverley* is Balzac's first completed novel, *The Chouans* (1829). The far-flung spot, the journey, the go-between, the encounter with the leader, even the details of an ambush – all are re-assembled in an interpretation of the Chouan rising in the Britanny of 1799 in which the rising is partly attributed to the simultaneity of the non-simultaneous.

Closest of all to *Waverley*, however, is Pushkin's *The Captain's Daughter* (1836). Here, the protagonist's accompanied journey to the edge of civilization in the Steppe, then over the edge into the Pugachev Rebellion of 1773, to a meeting with its leader, to a supposed defection, to court martial, to a traumatic return to a ravaged home – all to the accompaniment of his retainer's remonstrations – is in service of the theme 'Heaven send that we may never see such another senseless and merciless rebellion *à la russe*!'

It would be wrong to portray such works as drab *Waverley* look-alikes. Tieck's theme is not cultural but religious tolerance, the idea, familiar to Romantic theology, that 'many paths can lead to the Lord'. Balzac's go-between, the modern-thinking courtesan Mlle de Verneuil, gives his work a passion Scott never attains. And both Balzac and Pushkin shed Scott's decorum to render far more of the horror of rebellion. On the other hand, it would be wrong also to conceal Scott's superiority: none of them attains Scott's broad canvas; none of them can pen in the minor character; none of them is anything like as full of world. As Pushkin himself wrote: 'In our time, by the term "novel" we mean an historical epoch developed in a fictional narrative. Walter Scott attracted a whole crowd of imitators. But how far they all are from the Scottish wonder-worker!'

A further mark of *Waverley*'s stature, however, is that its influence is not confined to such imitations: Edward's journeys from central power to periphery and his experiences at Prestonpans have another progeny. From Stendhal's Fabrice at Waterloo in *The Charterhouse of Parma* (1839) to Tolstoy's Pierre at Borodino in *War and Peace* (1865–9) to Galdós's I-narrator in *Trafalgar* (1880), authors repeatedly send their anti-heroes into the reality of the modern battlefield. And from Balzac's *Colonel Chabert* (1832) and Rellstab's *1812* (1834) to Erckmann-Chatrian's *History of an 1813 Conscript* (1864), they send them foot-slogging the new distances of the new dispensations. If, as Scott wrote in 1824, 'The Muse of Fiction has considerably extended her walk' (Williams, 298), it was not least he himself who enlarged her ambit.

And equally, all over Europe and beyond – be it under the impact of *Waverley* or of the Waverley Novels – national literatures are being enriched by their first historical novels. In France, by Hugo and de Vigny; in Germany, by Alexis and Hauff; in Hungary, by Jósika; in Italy, by Grossi and Manzoni; in Portugal, by Herculano and Garrett; in Spain, by Espronceda and Larra; in Russia, by Zagoskin and Lazheechnikov; in Switzerland, by Zschokke; in Canada, by John Richardson; in America (where *Waverley* became available in 1815) by Fenimore Cooper. Nor is that the end of it. Given that Cooper's *The Spy* is seen not only as the first American historical novel but as the first 'American' novel at all, and Washington Irving's *Rip van Winkle* – also profoundly marked by *Waverley*'s sense of social change – as the first American short story, the extraordinary impact of Scott's own first novel can be sensed. For as America, so Europe: whether the historical novels of Balzac, Pushkin, Tieck and the like are Scott look-alikes or not, their own marked impact on their own national literatures must also go in part to *Waverley*'s account.

In a period and genre so much under Scott's sway, it is easy to overlook any advance on his achievement – and yet two there were, and remarkably early. Fenimore Cooper's *The Pioneers; or, The Sources of the Susquehanna* (1823) and Alessandro Manzoni's *The Betrothed* (1827) may draw on many Scott devices, but both offer a creative re-working of his theme of time conflict. As his title and subtitle suggest Cooper's central conflict is between the New England settlers with their watch-words 'time is money', 'time and tide wait for no man' and the richly wooded and rivered foothills of the Alleghenies, with their quite different time-rhythms. As the woods are plundered, Judge Temple sounds a note of lastness hardly present in Scott: 'I earnestly beg you will remember, that they are the growth of centuries, and when once gone, none living will see their loss remedied.' In *Redgauntlet*, the seining of rivers is an incident: in *The Pioneers* it is an integral part of a grand ecological theme – 'use, but don't waste'. Similarly, it was left to Manzoni and his splendid Fra Cristoforo to unite in one work the concerns of the Age of History with the Age of the Theodicy, which it eclipsed. Through the friar's vision that 'Time is His, and He has promised us so much of it' the historical comedy of lovers united becomes the sovereign comedy of a world held in God's hand.

Scott's eclipse starts at different times in differing countries and movements but by the 1860s his period of sway is past: Mérimée is now disparaging, Tolstoy virtually silent. Nevertheless, *War and Peace* is a working out of the theme of two lives present in the structure of *Waverley* and reflected on in subsequent works. 'I will not', writes Darsie in *Redgauntlet*, '– indeed I feel myself incompetent to argue a question of such metaphysical subtlety, as that which involves the limits betwixt free-will and predestination' (*RG* 8). But that is just what Tolstoy so magnificently does in his excursus and epilogues.

'With Scott', wrote F. R. Leavis in his one remark on him, tucked away in a footnote in *The Great Tradition* (1948), 'a bad tradition began.' Cooper, Balzac, Pushkin, Stendhal, Gogol, Thackeray, Tolstoy, Galdós ...: some tradition, some badness! If the sociology of the historical novel sketched in chapter 1 is at all correct, then the genre would have arisen in a changing Europe even if there had been no changing Scotland and changing Scott. Without the impetus amd stimulus of *Waverley*, however, it would have arisen later, different and less rich.

26 The influence on European realism

It is the object of the novel-writer to place before the reader as full and accurate representation of the events as can be done ...

Lives of the Novelists: 'Henry Fielding'

To appreciate a further legacy of *Waverley*, it is perhaps best to return to the early reviews, which are virtually unanimous in praising Scott for 'minute delineation', for a 'picture drawn from life', for a 'faithful picture', for 'felicity in delineation', for 'accuracy' and 'consistency', for having produced in short, as the *Monthly Review* claimed, 'as correct, minute, and spirited a copy of nature as ever came from the hands of an artist'. Comparisons with the visual arts abound, the *Quarterly Review* comparing Scott to 'a Teniers or Gerard Dow', and almost all reviewers praise, and quote at length, one of two passages: Edward's approach to Tully-Veolan through the squalor of its village or the 'still life' of the House itself. Their enthusiasm is justified – there is nothing like this in the European novel for more than a decade, perhaps two. But thereafter, such writing is the mode and Scott, often the model.

'Minuteness' (18) and 'accuracy' (60) are words Scott himself uses to characterize his descriptions in *Waverley*; he also depicts himself there and in the Advertisement of 1829 as a painter. In such passages and in his several reviews, essays and introductions to *Ballantyne's Novelists Library* (1821–4), Scott gradually moves forward to an aesthetic which in the mid-1820s, in a piece on Defoe, he expresses as follows:

> The air of writing with all the plausibility of truth must, in almost every case, have its own particular value; as we admire the paintings of some Flemish artists, where, though the subjects drawn are mean and disagreeable, and such as in nature we would not wish to study or look close upon, yet the skill with which they are represented by the painter gives an interest to the imitation upon canvas which the original entirely wants. (Williams, 179)

This linking of common life, *genre* painting and the novel was destined to become for some thirty years and more the watchword and apologia of a new generation of novelists across Europe – the realists. Asked what constitutes the worth of a novelist, they would reply, as did Scott on Defoe, that 'it is chiefly to be ascribed to the unequalled dexterity with which our author has given an appearance of REALITY to the incidents which he narrates' (Williams, 172).

It is helpful to distinguish with Damian Grant between 'conscientious realism', which undertakes painstakingly to create a simulacrum of the external world, and 'conscious realism', which stresses not the simulacrum but the creation, the achievement of something which does not exist *a priori*. Given that distinction, it is not least the 'conscientious realism' of Scott and *Waverley* which was seminal – above all for Balzac's *Comédie humaine*, but also for a host of major authors from Pushkin to Fontane. Their many homages to Scott can be represented in perhaps the earliest – Victor Hugo's excited cry in a review of Scott in 1819: 'Ineptness is blind: talent observes; and in truth, that's all the difference.'

One striking and influential aspect of Scott's observational realism in *Waverley* is his use, both in narrative and, especially, in dialogue, of Scots – Scots vocabulary, spelling and even grammar. The use is not thoroughgoing: Scots vocabulary in narrative occurs infrequently, and as with 'hallan' (50), 'hanchman' (75), 'bladier' (75), 'lofted house' (93), 'strath' (59) and even 'glen' (59) and 'bhaird' (75) tends to be immediately followed by an English explanation. Nor is the use consistent: in dialogue, Bradwardine fluctuates between greater or lesser use of it, and no character's speech is given solely in Scots. Nevertheless, the interplay of Scots and English does allow Scott to portray a further reality of his changing and divided country, where the Lowlands gentry and clergy such as Melville and Morton speak English, but the lower classes such as Mrs Flockhart broad Scots, where in a family such as the Bradwardines the father speaks a medley, but the daughter only English, and where a highlander such as Evan Dhu can modulate from English into Scots into Highland Scots and then into Gaelic.

The use of dialect, however, is only one of many identifying marks of the nineteenth-century historical novel which result from this representational proclivity: the precision tags 'of these times', 'of this period', the rendering of folk sayings and proverbs, the cataloguing of national custom, the elucidatory footnotes, the very periods of prose in commodious volumes, the suffusing aura of thinginess – all are first found in *Waverley*. As Alan Massie justly wrote, Scott 'showed something of the load of fact the novel could bear' (Bold, 106).

Of course, there is also 'conscious realism' in *Waverley*, and more in *Redgauntlet*. But one of the nice congruities of Scott's first novel is that just as its style is freighted down with world, so the conscious imaginings of its protagonist are finally tethered to the tent-pins of the possible. J. P. Stern memorably argued that 'Realism in life and literature alike depends upon a balance between mind and world, inner and outer, at a certain point in time' (142). It is that balance, at times precarious in his own life, which Scott strove to achieve in his work.

27 The influence on nineteenth-century historiography

'ye're gude seekers but ill finders'

The Antiquary, XXIII

'But Scott's greatest influence on the intellectual life of Europe was not immediate, in fiction: it was indirect, through the historical philosophy which underlay his novels and which, by them, he popularized. If any one man made the difference between the historians of the eighteenth and those of the nineteeth century, it was he' (Bell, 1971, 30). Lord Dacre's words remind one that *Waverley* and the genre it launched are one of the best examples of how the creative writer can anticipate and influence an academic discipline – even one which does not emerge from his work unscathed: history.

Some of the constituents needed to grasp this influence have already been assembled: Scott's sense for the qualitative difference between past and present; his ability to feel his way back despite that difference; his sense of the past as an intermeshed whole; his awareness of a social past alongside and beneath a political. The other constituents are found here, there and everywhere in the essays and *obiter dicta* of Europe's leading historians – avowals of an admiration for Scott in historians as different from him and from each other as Macaulay, Thierry, Ranke and Carlyle, all of whom then work out that admiration in their historical writings.

To chart this influence is more problematic: the topoi to be mapped are more nebulous, the histories of history with sufficient scope and depth have yet to be written. Perhaps the best way for the English reader to follow the pattern of influence is to read Macaulay's essay 'History' (1828), or Carlyle's 'On History' (1830) and 'On History Again' (1833), and then to read the respective history which ensues.

Macaulay begins from the perception of an absence – 'We are acquainted with no history which approaches our notion of what a history ought to be' – and proceeds to sketch in an historian of the future who knows that 'facts are the mere dross of history', who has 'an imagination sufficiently powerful to make his narrative affecting and picturesque', who recognizes that 'the upper current of society presents no certain criterion by which we can judge of the direction in which the under current flows', who does not think it beneath his dignity to 'dwell on the details which constitute the charm of biography', who, in short, does not 'look at past times as princes look at foreign countries'. Macaulay, in other words, plays Edward-Scott to the Bradwardine of prior history.

And when Macaulay subsequently opens his *History of England* (1848–61), with the proclamation that 'It will be my endeavour to relate the history of the people as well as the history of the government, to trace the progress of useful and ornamental arts, to describe the rise of religious sects and the changes of literary taste, to portray the manners of successive generations, and not to pass by with neglect the revolutions which have taken place in dress, furniture, repasts, and public amusements', he is beginning a history as inconceivable before Scott as it was imperative after. No part of Macaulay's programme can startle us today, but the very acceptability of it is a double reminder that history too has its past, and that in these respects history has become what the historical novel was.

28 *Waverley* as bestseller

to the mart of literature ... *The Bride of Lammermoor*, I

There is no point in being squeamish about it: Scott was a flagrant exception to the adage that genius should be born but not paid. 'From the first dawn of letters, in fact, up to the present time, there is' – the *Dumfries Courier* could claim in 1832 – 'no instance of an author who was at once so celebrated and able to turn his celebrity to so good account.' Already unprecedentedly successful as a poet, Scott was launched by *Waverley* into an equally unprecedented career as bestselling novelist. The sales are an index of his closeness to the pulse of his age. They are the precondition of his influence in letters and history, or at least of an influence so swift and far-flung. But they are also more.

The dates and data are well established and can be easily recapitulated. The first edition of *Waverley* published on 7 July 1814 – 1,000 copies priced at one guinea – was selling so well by the end of July that a second edition of 2,000 copies was planned, soon to be followed in October and November by a third and fourth. Within half a year 6,000 copies had changed hands, so that *Waverley* was the bestselling novel in England in 1814.

Striking as these data are, however, they should not be allowed to obscure others of equal significance. One guinea was no normal price for a three-volume novel: Jane Austen's *Mansfield Park*, published in three volumes just a month earlier, cost 18*s*., and 15*s*. was also a common figure. In order to sell a novel at such a sum, Scott's publisher, Archibald Constable, launched an advertising campaign: the work was announced in the *Edinburgh Weekly Journal*, the *Edinburgh Correspondent* and the *Edinburgh Advertiser* in late June 1814, and in regional papers such as the *Glasgow Courier* and *Perth Courier* in mid July, with notices in London papers following at the end of the month. Announcements were often central front page, at times with target booksellers named. And to this Scott added his own touch: the cloak of anonymity may have resulted from his own reluctance to espouse the novel as genre; or from his love of a persona; but it also gave the work an added piquancy. Recalling the 'electric shock of delight' which the newness of *Waverley* produced in Edinburgh and remarking that, 'Except the first opening of the *Edinburgh Review*, no work that has appeared in my time made such an instant and universal impression', Henry Cockburn adds: 'If the concealment of the authorship was intended to make mystery heighten their effect, it completely succeeded. The speculations and conjectures, and nods and winks, and predictions and assertions were endless, and occupied every company, and almost every two men who met and spoke in the street' (270–1).

One must be careful not to overstate the matter. Scouring the Edinburgh papers of the day one finds no reference to the stir *Waverley* caused. Browsing in the literary diaries and journals of the time one finds assiduous readers – such as

Lord Broughton and Elizabeth Wynne – who give no indication of having read it. Nevertheless, *Waverley* certainly did issue its *tolle, lege* to many and was read by Byron on appearance, by Jane Austen, Maria Edgeworth and Carlyle by autumn 1814, by Crabb Robinson and Wordsworth the following spring and by Mary Shelley three times between 1815 and 1821. In such circles the response is well expressed by a letter from Carlyle to Robert Mitchell in October 1814: 'Give me your opinion of it if you have read it, and if not, endeavour by all means to procure it.'

The procuring of *Waverley*, however, had only just begun. In the years following, Scott also wrote the bestselling novel – *Guy Mannering* in 1815, *The Antiquary* in 1816 and *Rob Roy* in 1818, each of them outstripping the early success of its predecessor – but sales of *Waverley* held up so well as to justify further editions in 1815, 1816, 1817 and 1821. By that time it was also selling in *The Novels and Tales of the Author of Waverley*, five editions of which appeared between 1819 and 1825. And yet for all this, in 1829 *Waverley* still had it in it to re-emerge as a bestseller in an 'Author's Edition of the Waverley Novels' – the so-termed 'Magnum Edition' at 5*s*. a volume – where it sold 40,000 more copies between 1829 and *c*. 1836, including 25,000 in the first fortnight. This total of some 60,000 copies in just over twenty years includes neither the copies sold in the several American editions nor those in any of the European translations – yet it dwarfs the sales of Scott's contemporaries in England or abroad. By mid-1829, Cadell, Scott's new publisher, could justly write, cock-a-hoop, 'All former bookselling success is a joke to this.'

Paradoxically, *Waverley*'s success was not always to its benefit. The Magnum Edition of 1829 was based on an interleaved annotated version of all the novels to date, which Scott was coaxed into making by his printers and over which he toiled in his last years. Now, the outcome is a fascinating and moving record of Scott the historian and antiquarian editing Scott the novelist; it contains some sensitive emendations to the text; it is full of illumination on Scott's sources and hence his method of composition; and in the case of *Waverley* it appends two earlier forays into historical fiction. But it has meant also that from 1829 until the 1970s readers invariably encountered *Waverley* not only via its own introductory chapter 1 and own 1829 introduction, but via the introduction to the entire Magnum Edition and its three lengthy appendices to boot – an approach to which the sanest reaction would be that of Mowbray in *St Ronan's Well*: 'Remember, I hate prefaces; and when I happen to open a book always skip them' (*SR* 11).

Nor, one suspects, has it helped *Waverley* that its publishing success and that of the Waverley Novels continued long beyond 1836. The Magnum Edition sold a further 38,000 sets up to 1849, a People's Edition of the Waverley Novels moved over 8 million weekly numbers from 1855, and as the copyrights expired, so successively cheaper editions appeared, at 1*s*. a volume in 1862–3, then at 6*d*., then at 3*d*. *Waverley* is therefore often first encountered in a place not always suited to enhancing its appreciation – the second-hand bookstore.

To glimpse it there, however, is to gain a glimpse of publishing history. Here is the first major modern novel to be thrustfully marketed, to capture a large readership, to succeed as a recent fiction reprint, to command its price and to enrich both its genre and its author. There is a nice irony in the fact that a novel published anonymously partly because its author was reluctant to assume the ill-reputed mantle of novelist should become a landmark also in the establishing of novel-writing as a profession. With *Waverley*, the novel leaves the garret *en route* for Abbotsford.

Chapter 5

Conclusions

29 A fourfold landmark of world literature

His works possess the rare and invaluable property of originality, to which all other qualities are as dust in the balance

Lives of the Novelists: 'Henry Mackenzie'

Waverley is not a work without flaw: it does contain weaknesses in the characterization of Edward and Rose; it does reveal missed opportunities when compared with its immediate successors in the genre; there is (as often in Scott) an undue haste in its conclusion; and, yes, *il y a des longueurs*. But whatever criterion of literary greatness one applies apart from artistic perfection, *Waverley* stands the test.

No work of literature will survive, Erich Heller once said, unless it has a 'syntax of ideas' underpinning it. *Waverley* has such a syntax, indeed two syntaxes. There is the constellation of themes concerned with social relationships in a world where the old familiarities and co-ordinates are being swept away by change – relationships between yesterday and tomorrow, 'primitive' and 'civilized', periphery and centre, nationhood and empire. And there is the constellation of ideas concerned with how those yesterdays are to be recollected, with what constitutes the right depository for the worlds we have lost.

A classic, Frank Kermode has argued, is a work which transcends provincial boundaries. Few works of European literature have done that so resoundingly, its themes providing a new structure of self-understanding and its form and manner providing a new mode of writing for virtually all the emergent national literatures of Europe and for many who were to become the nineteenth century's most eminent novelists.

Great works of art, T.S. Eliot wrote in 'Tradition and the Individual Talent' (1919), 'form an ideal order among themselves, which is modified by the introduction of the new (the really new) work of art among them'. And he adds, 'we do not quite say that the new is more valuable because it fits in; but its fitting in is a test of its value'. The clearest mark of *Waverley*'s quality is that it fits in to our stories of the historical novel as genre, of European realism, of the development of historiography and of novel-publishing. In these four stories, moreover, it has its place not only in England but in a large number of other national literatures – and, as befits the newness of *Waverley*, it is often a place which marks a beginning. Scott, the great novelist of lastness, has too much firstness about him for that place ever to be gainsaid.

Waverley, in other words, is not just a landmark of world literature but a fourfold landmark. Indeed, when Goethe first coined the term *Weltliteratur*, it was, among others, to the author of *Waverley* that he was referring.

30 Scott, the verbal museum and us

Remove not the old land-mark, and enter not into the fields of the fatherless *Letters of Malachi Malagrowther*, II

But what of now – now, when, as critics never tire of remarking, 'tis not just sixty, but a good many more years since; now, when the bagpipes and didgeridoo alike are played by buskers on the streets of our capital cities; now when everything from the highland croft to the lowland spinning mill is being rescued into or converted into a museum; now when in social change and cultural decay, centralization and nationalism developments are moving at such a pace that the stream of time depicted by Scott has become a racing torrent; now when the genre *Waverley* inaugurated, the historical novel, has repeatedly been declared passé. Is not *Waverley* now *itself* a victim of the process it portrays, not now *itself* confined to the status of museum-piece?

It is the hallmark of *Waverley*'s quality that the answer to this question is both firmly 'Yes' and firmly 'No'. Yes, *Waverley* is a literary landmark, its role in our narratives of world literature, our literary-historical museums, assured. But no, *Waverley* is not one of those cases where yesterday's landmark is today's eyesore.

Of course, there is no denying the fall in Scott's overall appreciation from the dizzy heights of the early 1820s or 1832: it fell as the attention of literature turned to urbanization, industry and Empire; fell as he himself scot(t)ched his reputation through his latter and lesser works; fell as he too, like many innovators, could not be saved from his disciples; fell with the tendency to make erstwhile penury a criterion for present significance and textual difficulty the preferred occasion for critical triumph. But with an oeuvre as large and a readership as vast as Scott's, statements on overall reputation are neither very informative nor very reliable. Scott's Scottish novels have never lacked their appreciators, perhaps because the issues they raise have never been resolved, only (at times) eclipsed. Indeed, Scott's overall reputation fell not least as he himself fell victim to the process he so memorably portrayed: as his country was marginalized so was he too marginalized.

Today, neither of the two constellations of themes on which *Waverley* rests has lost any of its timeliness. *Waverley* is a landmark not least because it is itself *about* landmarks – and hence directly apposite to our own relationship with the worlds we have lost, to our losing them with increasing rapidity by the year, and to our counting the human cost of the transition. The faster our worlds change, the more we are surrounded by examples of Bradwardinism and Evan Dhus, the more we find ourselves caught as wavering Edwards between old and new, the more we not only recognize Scott as a landmark, but recognize his recognition of the need for landmarks. Paraphrasing Scott we might say: 'If you uproot us, you will find us damned mischievous citizens.' And as the uprooting and mischief gather pace, the farther he is from us, the closer he is to us.

Equally timely are the themes concerned with empire and nationhood. Not only has Scotland still fully to resolve its tensions between periphery and centre, but it is by no means the only country to have still to do so. Modern society at large has been described as one of a macro-stability in which micro-instabilities are continually sacrificed to the whole, and *Waverley* is the first novel to portray the sacrifice in process.

Of the continuing appositeness of *Waverley* there are clear tokens also within literature and literary criticism. The historical novel, far from being moribund, has suffered only the fate of premature obituary, which it shares with other genres equally alive and well. One has only to mention the names of Thomas Mann, Lampedusa, Richard Hughes, Solzhenitsyn, Patrick White, Chinua Achebe and Golding, to see that the genre has flourished in the post-1945 world. The *temps des musées* has been superseded by the 'museological explosion' of our own era: never, we are told, has there been a present as past-oriented as our own. And in our museum culture the verbal museum of the historical novel continues to be much frequented.

To be sure, there is one aspect of our century of horrors which makes it little suited to the *Waverley* scheme: about fascism, or Pol Pot or apartheid there is nothing bonnie, and where there is nothing bonnie there can be no wavering. Where such an attempt is made, as in Andersch's *Winterspelt* (1974), it lacks the ability to grip and tease.

Even in the case of the Third Reich, however, Hughes's magnificent Augustus in *The Human Predicament* (1961–73) shows that Waverley as traveller, if not as waverer, is still a valid and rewarding plot gambit, and elsewhere – in Lampedusa (a great Scott reader), Achebe, Ngugi, White and Farrell – there are repeated examples of much more of the *Waverley* pattern being applicable to the (often colonial) reality portrayed.

And as in literature, so in literary criticism. It is still possible to hear professors and pundits alike pontificating on Scott without having read him. But their neglect has brought others the rewards of re-discovery. Vigorous research has re-asserted much of Scott's quality, and there are now excellent editions available, with the new Edinburgh Edition on the horizon.

The way an age preserves the presence of its past is an important index of its own present condition. The renewed presence both of the historical novel and of the *Waverley* model in our literatures and literary criticism is a pointer to the striking parallels between Scott's age and our own. The Europe of a few years back? – *Ah! parlez-moi d'Adam et d'Eve.* Superstate or nationhood, centralism or federalism? – Topics of pressing concern. Perhaps this is why, in Old World and New, today's students almost invariably respond to Scott with surprise and appreciation, finding, rather as Byron did in July 1814, that '*Waverley* is the best and most interesting novel I have read since – I don't know when.'

Appendix
Contemporary Accounts of the Battle of Prestonpans (21 September 1745)

(Orthography and punctuation have been left completely unchanged)

A

Anon,

A Compleat and Authentick History of the Rise, Progress, and Extinction of the Late Rebellion and of the Proceedings Against the Principal Persons Concerned Therein (London, 1747)

They attacked the King's Troops about Three in the Morning, and the Dragoons breaking on the first Fire, left the Foot exposed to the *Highlanders*, by whom, after a short Dispute, they were defeated, a considerable Number killed, and the best Part of the rest made Prisoners, the few Field-Pieces they had with them being likewise taken. The Earls of *Loudon* and *Hume* having rallied the Dragoons, retired with them to *Lauder*, and from thence the next Day to *Berwick*; Brigadier *Fowke*, and Col. *Lascelles* came back to *Dumbar*, and Sir *John Cope* went to *Berwick*. This is, by some called the Battle of *Preston Pans*, by others the Battle of *Seaton*, from two little Towns near which it is fought; but if it must be stiled a Battle, it is more properly the Battle of *Glaidesmuir*, since that was the Field of Battle, being a wide barren Heath, about seven Miles East from *Edinburgh*. (7–8)

[There follows a list of the officers killed on the Hanoverian side.]

B

Michael Hughes

A Plain Narrative or Journal of the late Rebellion begun in 1745 describing its Progress in Scotland and England till the full and glorious Defeat at Culloden (London, 1746)

The Rebels began their Fire upon the Dragoons, which put them first into Disorder, they not returning the Fire once, or obeying the Word of Command. It was the Horse turning back that first caused the Foot to be in Confusion, and bad Commanders make bad Soldiers. The Firing did not last above Five Minutes before they came to the Sword in Hand, and then it caused a general Confusion among Officers and Soldiers; for the King's Men were somewhat surprised at the Manner of the *Highlander*'s Behaviour in the Attack. However, after seizing the Train, and the sudden Flight of our dragoons, the Enemy soon broke the Ranks, killed and wounded many of the King's Men and made many Prisoners. General *Cope* escaped to the Sea-Side, and made off to *Berwick* with about four hundred and fifty Dragoons. The rest of the Officers and Men dispersed different Ways about the Country. With us Colonel *Lee*'s Regiment of Foot and some others did pretty much Execution among the Rebels before they broke in.

After the Battel was over, the Conquerors began to look after *Johnny Cope*'s Equipage, Tent-furniture, and what other Spoil they could pick up; when they soon found all the General's Baggage and great Riches, at least to them. They got by this Defeat Arms, and Ammunition, and other warlike Stores. *Cope*'s Men were not in a Country which is frequently the Seat of War, tho' they might be well exercised and trained soldiers: So is a Mathematician in the Art of Navigation, but when he comes to Sea he is at a little Loss for want of Trial and Experience. A few *Flanders* Regiments of ours, with a good Commander, would have disputed the Cause much better with them. (13–14)

C

The Caledonian Mercury
23 September 1745. By Authority

The Signal having been given to form and attack, nothing could parallel the Celerity and Dextrousness with which the Highlanders performed that Motion, except the Courage and Ardour with which they afterwards fought, and pulling off their Bonnets, looking up to Heaven, made a short Prayer, and run forward. They received a very full Fire from Right to Left of the Enemy, which killed severals; but advancing up, they discharged and threw down their Muskets, and drawing their broad swords, gave a most frightful and hideous Shout, rushing most furiously upon the Enemy, so that in 7 or 8 Minutes, both Horse and Foot were totally routed and drove from the Field of Battle; though it must be owned that the Enemy fought very gallantly, but they could not withstand the Impetuosity, or rather Fury of the Highlanders, and were forced to *run* when they could no longer *resist*.

Some Dragoons formed soon after on a neighbouring Eminence, but observing our men marching to attack them, fled to Dalkeith, others took Shelter in the neighbouring Villages, others again got to Leith; Major Cawfield rode up to the Castle of Edinburgh, and was followed by a few Dragoons, who discharged their load Pistols at People in the Street. We know not what became of General Cope, are only informed that he escaped in a Boat, and got aboard the Fox Man of War.

As the second Line, which was commanded by the Lord Nairn, and consisted of the Athole Men, Strowan's People, the Macklachlans, &c. could not come up to have a share of the Honour, and the Nobility, Gentry, &c. stood on Horseback, as a Reserve, it may in Justice be said, That 2000 Highland Foot, unsupported by Horse, and charged in Front and Flank with Artillery and small Arms, routed a regular Army of above 4000 Horse and Foot in an open Plain, and obtained a most signal and complete victory with a very inconsiderable Loss.

We had killed on the Spot in this Battle of Gladsmuir near Seton House

[list of 5 officers]
And about 30 private Men, and 70 or 80 wounded.
On the other Hand the Enemy had killed
[list of enemy officers killed, then wounded]

'Tis computed about 500 of the Enemy were killed; and that 900 are wounded, and that we have taken about 1400 Prisoners. All their Cannon, Mortars, several Colours, Standards, Abundance of Horses and Arms were taken. As was all their Baggage, Equipage &c.

The Prince, as soon as Victory declared for him, mounted his Horse and put a Stop to the Slaughter; and finding no Surgeons amongst the Enemy, dispatched an Officer to Edinburgh with Orders to bring all the Surgeons to attend; which was accordingly done.

Guide to further reading

Scott's works

Waverley contains its own caution to readers of fiction. Nevertheless, the reader attracted to the issues raised in *Waverley* may well wish to pursue them first in Scott's other Scottish novels and shorter pieces – notably in *Rob Roy, The Heart of Midlothian, Redgauntlet, Old Mortality* and *The Antiquary*; and in *The Two Drovers* and *The Highland Widow*. All are readily available in paperback, although the devotee may prefer the Border Edition (ed. Andrew Lang, 1892–4) or the Dryburgh Edition (1892–4). The first ever critical edition of Scott's works – the Edinburgh Edition – is now underway, but has yet to appear. Largely less accessible until then but also rewarding for the light they throw on Scott's mind and times are the works listed in the prefatory Note.

Autobiographical material

One of the best ways into Scott's mind is through the catalogue of his remarkable library. Another is through his voluminous correspondence, now admirably annotated by James C. Corson. The most significant autobiographical writings have been gathered and excellently introduced by Hewitt, and the best literary-critical pieces given equal treatment by Williams. The magnificent *Journal* covers the final years from November 1825 but also contains reflections on Scott's earlier life and craft.

Anderson, W.E.K., ed., *The Journal of Sir Walter Scott*, Oxford University Press, 1972

Cochrane, J.G., *Catalogue of the Library at Abbotsford*, Edinburgh, 1838, reprinted Johnson Reprint Corp., New York, 1971

Corson, James C., *Notes and Index to Sir Herbert Grierson's Edition of the Letters of Sir Walter Scott*, Oxford University Press, 1979

Grierson, H.J.C., ed., *The Letters of Sir Walter Scott*, 12 vols., Constable, London, 1932–7

Hewitt, David, ed., *Scott on Himself: A Selection of the Autobiographical Writings of Sir Walter Scott*, Scottish Academic Press, Edinburgh, 1981

Williams, Ioan, ed., *Sir Walter Scott on Novelists and Fiction*, Barnes and Noble, New York, 1968

Biography

Scott has received the biographers he richly deserves. Lockhart is indispensable though not always reliable. Johnson's is a magnificently detailed account. Buchan, Daiches, Grierson and Wilson all blend the enthusiastic with the dispassionate. Cockburn and Mackintosh offer valuable reflections of contemporaries. The Bicentenary Exhibition catalogue, still available, is perhaps the best short introduction to the man, his world and work.

Bell, A. S., ed., *Sir Walter Scott 1771–1971: A Bicentenary Exhibition*, HMSO, Glasgow, 1971

Buchan, John, *Sir Walter Scott*, Cassell, London, 1932

Cockburn, Henry, *Memorials of His Time*, ed. Harry Cockburn, Foulis, Edinburgh and London, 1909

Daiches, David, *Sir Walter Scott and His World*, Thames and Hudson, London, 1971

Grierson, H. J. C., *Sir Walter Scott, Bart.*, Constable, London, 1938

Johnson, Edgar, *Sir Walter Scott: The Great Unknown*, 2 vols., Macmillan, New York, 1970

Lockhart, J. G., *Memoirs of the Life of Sir Walter Scott, Bart.*, 7 vols., Edinburgh, 1837–8; abridged versions available

Mackintosh, R. J., ed., *Memoirs of the Life of Sir James Mackintosh*, London, 1835

Wilson, A. N., *The Laird of Abbotsford: A View of Sir Walter Scott*, Oxford University Press, 1989

Editions of *Waverley*

Waverley is currently available in Everyman paperback (ed. James C. Corson, London, 1969), as a Penguin Classic (ed. Andrew Hook, Harmondsworth, 1972) and in the Oxford University Press World's Classics series (ed. Claire Lamont, Oxford 1986). All three editions have useful glossary material; those of Hook and Lamont have both lively and instructive introductions and helpful annotations; Lamont's edition, based on her prize-winning Clarendon Press edition of 1981, also preserves the original three-volume structure and is rich but discreet in its notes. Hook offers the Magnum Opus text of 1829, Lamont that of 1814 (in each case corrected from manuscript). A brief and sensitive introduction to the textual issues involved is found in the review of the Lamont edition below.

Alexander, J. H., review of Claire Lamont's Clarendon edition (1981) of *Waverley, Scottish Literary Journal*, Supplement no. 17, winter 1982

Early critical responses

The changing response to the Waverley Novels (up to the 1930s) has been best traced by Hillhouse, that to Scott in general (up to the 1880s) by Hayden. It is still, however, worth looking up the earliest reviews, which are listed in Hayden, pp. 542–3.

Hayden, John O., *Scott: The Critical Heritage*, Routledge and Kegan Paul, London, 1970

Hillhouse, James T., *The Waverley Novels and Their Critics*, Minnesota, 1936; reprinted Octagon Books, New York, 1970

Social and intellectual background

The changing socio-political world from which *Waverley* emerged has been well mapped on a European scale by Hobsbawm and on a Scottish scale by Devine, Lenman and Smout; the corresponding charting of Scott's intellectual horizons has been nicely done by Becker and Talmon, Daiches and Forbes. As a study of the world of printing and literacy to which Scott is inextricably tied, Altick remains unparalleled.

Altick, Richard, *The English Common Reader*, Chicago University Press, 1957

Becker, Carl L., *The Heavenly City of the Eighteenth-Century Philosophers*, Yale University Press, New Haven, 1932

Daiches, David, *The Scottish Enlightenment: An Introduction*, The Saltire Society, Edinburgh, 1986

Devine, T. M., and Rosalind Mitchison, eds., *People and Society in Scotland 1760–1830*, John Donald, Edinburgh, 1988

Forbes, Duncan, 'The Rationalism of Walter Scott', *Cambridge Journal*, 7, 1 (1953), pp. 20–35

Hobsbawm, Eric, *The Age of Revolution 1789–1848*, Praeger Publications, New York, 1962

Nations and Nationalism Since 1780: Programme, Myth and Reality, Cambridge University Press, 1990

Lenman, Bruce, *Integration, Enlightenment, and Industrialization: Scotland 1746–1832*, Edward Arnold, London, 1981

Smout, T. C., *A History of the Scottish People 1560–1830*, Fontana/Collins, London, 1969

Smout, T. C., and Sydney Wood, eds., *Scottish Voices 1745–1960*, Collins, London, 1990

Talmon, J. L., *Romanticism and Revolt: Europe 1815–1848*, Harcourt, Brace and World, New York, 1967

The museum culture

The various dimensions of the *temps des musées* are well depicted in the works below, Ian Gordon Brown and Piggott being the authorities on antiquarianism, Hobsbawm and Ranger providing the seminal book on tradition-invention and Connerton and Lübbe supplying the sociological and philosophical glosses.

Brown, Ian Gordon, *The Hobby-Horsical Antiquary: A Scottish Character 1640–1830*, National Library of Scotland, Edinburgh, 1980

'Modern Rome and Ancient Caledonia: the Union and the Politics of Scottish Culture', *The History of Scottish Literature*, vol. II, *1660–1800*, ed. Andrew Hook, Aberdeen University Press, 1990, pp. 33–49

Connerton, Paul, *How Societies Remember*, Cambridge University Press, 1989

Hobsbawm, Eric, and Terence Ranger, eds., *The Invention of Tradition*, Cambridge University Press, 1984

Lübbe, Hermann, *Der Fortschritt und das Museum: über den Grund unseres Vergnügens an historischen Gegenständen*, Institute of Germanic Studies, London, 1982

Piggott, Stuart, *Ruins in a Landscape: Essays in Antiquarianism*, Edinburgh University Press, 1976

Plumb, J.H., *The Death of the Past*, Houghton Mifflin, Boston, 1970

Trevor-Roper, Hugh, 'The Invention of Tradition: The Highland Tradition of Scotland', in Hobsbawm and Ranger, eds., pp. 15–41

Compendia of essays

The following compendia (subsequently referred to by editor) all contain valuable approaches both to Scott in general and *Waverley* in particular.

Alexander, J.H., and David Hewitt, eds., *Scott and His Influence: The Papers of the Aberdeen Scott Conference, 1982*, Association for Scottish Literary Studies, Aberdeen, 1983

Bell, Alan, ed., *Scott Bicentenary Essays: Selected Papers Read at the Sir Walter Scott Bicentenary Conference*, Scottish Academic Press, Edinburgh, 1983

Bold, Alan, ed., *Sir Walter Scott: The Long-Forgotten Melody*, Vision and Barnes and Noble, London, 1983

Devlin, D. D., ed., *Walter Scott: Modern Judgements*, Macmillan, London, 1968

Renwick, W. L., ed., *Sir Walter Scott Lectures 1940–1948*, Edinburgh University Press, 1950

Scott and Scotland

The P. H. Scott/Edwin Muir argument is the classic statement of the two poles of the issue. Pittock is a stimulating and broad-based literary addition to the controversy. Harvie, Nairn and Reid place Scott in an even broader socio-historical ambit.

Harvie, Christopher, *Scotland and Nationalism: Scottish Society and Politics 1707–1977*, George Allen and Unwin, London, 1977
'Scott and the Image of Scotland', in Bold, ed., pp. 17–41

Muir, Edwin, *Scott and Scotland: The Predicament of the Scottish Writer*, Routledge, London, 1936

Nairn, Tom, *The Break-Up of Britain*, second, expanded edition, Verso, London, 1981

Pittock, Murray, *The Invention of Scotland: the Stuart Myth and the Scottish Identity*, Routledge, London, 1991

Reid, J.M., *Modern Scottish Literature*, The Saltire Society, Edinburgh, 1945

Scott, P.H., *Walter Scott and Scotland*, William Blackwood, Edinburgh, 1981

General studies of Scott

Of the many overall studies of Scott, the following are especially rewarding or useful on *Waverley* (relevant chapters, part-chapters or parts being given in brackets where appropriate).

Brown, David, *Walter Scott and the Historical Imagination*, Routledge and Kegan Paul, London, 1979 (chapter 1)

Cockshut, A.O.J., *The Achievement of Walter Scott*, New York University Press, 1969 (Part Two, chapter 1)

Crawford, Thomas, *Walter Scott*, Scottish Academic Press, Edinburgh, 1982 (chapters 4 and 5)

Cusac, Marion, *Narrative Structure in the Novels of Walter Scott*, Mouton, The Hague and Paris, 1969

Devlin, D.D., *The Author of Waverley: A Critical Study of Walter Scott*, Macmillan, London 1971 (chapter 3)

Hart, Frances, *Scott's Novels: The Plotting of Historical Survival*, University Press of Virginia, Charlottesville, 1966

Hewitt, David, 'Walter Scott', *The History of Scottish Literature*, vol. III, *Nineteenth Century*, ed. Douglas Gifford, Aberdeen University Press, 1988, pp. 65–87

Iser, Wolfgang, *The Implied Reader*, 1974 (chapter 4)

Kerr, James, *Fiction Against History: Scott as Storyteller*, Cambridge University Press, 1989 (chapters 1 and 2)

Kiely, Robert, *The Romantic Novel in England*, Harvard University Press, Cambridge, Mass., 1972 (chapter 7)

Macqueen, John, *The Rise of the Historical Novel: The Enlightenment and Scottish Literature*, Scottish Academic Press, Edinburgh, 1989 (chapter 2)

Millgate, Jane, *Walter Scott: The Making of the Novelist*, Edinburgh University Press, 1984 (chapter 3)

Watson, George, *The Story of the Novel*, Macmillan, London, 1979 (chapter 8)

Welsh, Alexander, *The Hero of the Waverley Novels*, Yale University Press, New Haven, 1963

Articles on *Waverley*

Among the many shorter pieces on or partly on *Waverley*, the following are of especial note:

Daiches, David, 'Scott's Achievement as a Novelist', *Nineteenth-Century Fiction*, 6 (1951), pp. 81–95 and 153–73; now in Devlin, pp. 33–62

Garside, P.D., '*Waverley*'s Pictures of the Past', *English Literary History*, 44 (1977), pp. 659–82

'Scott, the Eighteenth Century and the New Man of Sentiment', *Anglia*, 103 (1985), pp. 71–89

'Dating *Waverley*'s Early Chapters', *The Bibliotheck*, 13 (1986), pp. 61–81

Gordon, S. Stewart, '*Waverley* and the "Unified Design" ', *English Literary History*, 18 (1951), pp. 107–22; now in Devlin, pp. 71–83

Skroka, Kenneth M., 'Education in Walter Scott's *Waverley*', *Studies in Scottish Literature*, 15 (1980), pp. 139–164

The Forty-five

The current state of research into, and understanding of, the Forty-five can be found in Lenman and the other works below. It is still rewarding, however, to read contemporary accounts such as listed beneath.

Lenman, Bruce, *The Jacobite Cause*, Richard Drew, Glasgow, 1986

The Jacobite Risings in Britain 1689–1746, Methuen, London, 1980

Livingstone, Alastair of Bachuil, Christian W. H. Aikman and Betty Stuart Hart, eds., *Muster Roll of Prince Charles Edward Stuart's Army 1745–46*, Aberdeen University Press, 1984

Scott-Moncrieff, Lesley, ed., *The '45: To Gather an Image Whole*, Mercat Press, Edinburgh, 1988

Tomasson, Katherine, and Francis Burt, *Battles of the '45*, Batsford, London, 1962

Carlyle, Alexander, *Autobiography*, in J.G. Fyfe, ed., *Scottish Diaries and Memoirs 1550–1746*, Stirling, n.d.

Lord Elcho, David, *A Short Account of the Affairs of Scotland in the Years 1744, 1745, 1746*, in J.G. Fyfe ed.

de Johnstone, Chevalier, *Memoirs of the Rebellion of 1745 and 1746*, London, 1820

Macpherson, James, *The History of the Present Rebellion in Scotland*, London, 1745

Ray, James, *A Compleat History of the Rebellion ...*, London, 1754

Volunteer, A, *Journey through Part of England and Scotland along with the Army under the Command of His Royal Highness the Duke of Cumberland ...*, London, 1747

On history

In the swiftly growing literature on the nature of history, and the role of narrative within both history and human self-understanding, the following stand out:

Bloch, Marc, *The Historian's Craft*, Random House, New York, 1953

Carr, E.H., *What Is History?*, Penguin, Harmondsworth, 1964

Collingwood, R.G., *The Idea of Nature*, Oxford University Press, 1945

The Idea of History, Oxford University Press, 1946

Danto, A.C., *Analytical Philosophy of History*, Cambridge University Press, 1965

Fain, Haskell, *Between Philosophy and History*, Princeton University Press, 1970

Gallie, W.B., *Philosophy and the Historical Understanding*, Shocken Books, New York, 1964

MacIntyre, Alasdair, *After Virtue: A Study in Moral Theory*, Duckworth, London, 1981 (chapter 15)

Oakeshott, Michael, *Experience and Its Modes*, Cambridge University Press, 1933 (chapter 3)

Scott and history

The relationship between Scott and the development of European historiography is explored in the following:

Anderson, James, *Sir Walter Scott and History*, Edina, Edinburgh, 1981

Butterfield, Sir Herbert, *Man on His Past: The Study of the History of Historical Scholarship*, Cambridge University Press, 1955

Carnall, Geoffrey, 'Historical Writing in the Later Eighteenth Century', *The History of Scottish Literature*, vol. II, *1660–1800*, ed. Andrew Hook, Aberdeen University Press, 1990, pp. 207–17

Philips, Mark, 'Macaulay, Scott, and the Literary Challenge to Historiography', *Journal of the History of Ideas*, 50 (1989), pp. 117–33

Trevor-Roper, Hugh, 'Sir Walter Scott and History', *The Listener*, 19 August 1971, pp. 225–32

Trevelyan, G.M., *Clio, a Muse and Other Essays*, Longmans, Green and Co., London, 1931

Wedgwood, C.V., *Truth and Opinion*, Collins, London, 1960

Realism and romance

The works below help to place *Waverley* between old romance and emergent realism.

Frye, Northrop, *The Anatomy of Criticism: Four Essays*, Princeton University Press, 1957

The Secular Scripture: A Study of the Structure of Romance, Harvard University Press, Cambridge, Mass., 1976

Grant, Damian, *Realism*, The Critical Idiom, Methuen, London, 1970

Harkin, Patricia, 'Romance and Real History: The Historical Novel as Literary Innovation', in Alexander and Hewitt, eds., pp. 157–168

Stern, J.P., *On Realism*, Concepts of Literature, Routledge and Kegan Paul, London, 1973

Watt, Ian, *The Rise of the Novel: Studies in Defoe, Richardson, Fielding*, Penguin, Harmondsworth, 1963

Influence in Europe and beyond

The impact of *Waverley*'s form and themes has long had its own impact upon comparatists. The following brief list perhaps does more justice to the former impact than to the latter.

Davie, Donald, *The Heyday of Sir Walter Scott*, Routledge and Kegan Paul, London, 1961

Dekker, George, *The American Historical Romance*, Cambridge University Press, 1987

Fleishman, Avrom, *The English Historical Novel: Walter Scott to Virginia Woolf*, Johns Hopkins Press, Baltimore and London, 1971

Humphrey, Richard, *The Historical Novel as Philosophy of History*, Institute of Germanic Studies, London, 1986 (chapters 1 and 2)

Lützeler, Paul Michael, 'Bürgerkriegsliteratur: Der historische Roman im Europa der Restaurationszeit (1815–1830)', in Jürgen Kocka, ed., *Bürgertum im 19. Jahrhundert*, Deutscher Taschenbuch Verlag, Munich, 1988, vol. III, pp. 232–56

Lukács, Georg, *Der historische Roman*, *Werke*, vol. VI, *Probleme des Realismus III*, Luchterhand, Neuwied, 1965; translated as *The Historical Novel* by Hannah and Stanley Mitchell, Penguin, Harmondsworth, 1962

Maigron, Louis, *Le roman historique à l'époque romantique*, Paris, 1898

Massie, Allan, 'Scott and the European Novel', in Bold, ed., pp. 91–106

Shaw, Harry E., *The Forms of Historical Fiction: Sir Walter Scott and His Successors*, Cornell University Press, Ithaca, 1983

More specifically, the influence in Canada, Denmark and Norway can be pursued in the essays of Bogaards, Nielsen and Tysdahl in Alexander and Hewitt, eds., and that in Italy, Hungary and Germany in the contributions of Jack, Katona and Ochojski to Bell, ed. (1983).

Teaching material

Finally, the following recent video-cassette can be a useful *point de départ* for teaching on Scott.

Hossick, Malcolm, *Walter Scott: A Concise Biography*, Famous Authors 12, Wonderland, 1991

Bibliographies

The above lists are intended for the interested reader or student. The researcher in need of detailed bibliographies of writing on Scott should turn to those of Corson (up to 1932) and Rubinstein (from 1932 to 1977). On research between 1970–4, the *Scottish Literary News*, and from 1974 the *Scottish Literary Journal* (Supplements) have provided excellent annual updates.

Corson, J.C., *A Bibliography of Sir Walter Scott*, Edinburgh, 1943

Rubinstein, Jill, *Sir Walter Scott: A Reference Guide*, Boston, 1978

For EU product safety concerns, contact us at Calle de José Abascal, 56–1°, 28003 Madrid, Spain or eugpsr@cambridge.org.

www.ingramcontent.com/pod-product-compliance
Ingram Content Group UK Ltd.
Pitfield, Milton Keynes, MK11 3LW, UK
UKHW012332130625
459647UK00009B/244

* 9 7 8 0 5 2 1 3 7 8 8 8 8 *